KV-370-036

Contents

CHECK YOUR TAX

AND
MONEY FACTS

2003–2004

by

GRAHAM M. KITCHEN, F.C.A.

Consultant Editors
CHRIS MADDOCK
and
KAREN FOSTER, A.T.T.
of BDO Stoy Hayward, Chartered Accountants

foulsham
LONDON • NEW YORK • TORONTO • SYDNEY

foulsham

The Publishing House, Bennetts Close,
Cippenham, Slough, Berkshire SL1 5AP, England

ISBN 0-572-02859-8

The tax forms reproduced in this book are
Crown copyright and printed with
permission of the Inland Revenue.

Printed in Great Britain by Creative Print & Design (Wales), Ebbw Vale.

CHAPTER 1

Budget summary

Although the changes proposed in the April 2003 budget and pre-budget report of November 2002 are dealt with throughout this book, this chapter summarises the main points and other relevant legislation that has occurred since the last edition, and gives references to the pages that deal specifically with each topic.

Personal allowances

The allowances for 2003–2004 are as follows:

	£	Page No.
Personal allowances:		
age under 65	4,615	68
age 65–74*	6,610	89
age 75 or over*	6,720	89
Married couple's allowance for those born before 6 April 1935:		
age 65–74*	5,565†	89
age 75 or over*	5,635†	89
minimum amount	2,150	89
Income limit*	18,300	89
Maintenance payment – maximum relief if born before 6 April 1935	2,150†	65
Blind person's allowance	1,510	69

†Relief at only 10 per cent.

Rates of tax

The income level for the 10 per cent tax band is increased to £1,960, with the 22 per cent band increased to £30,500. The higher rate of tax remains at 40 per cent.

The savings income tax rate and dividend rate remain unaltered for 2003-2004. — 139

Minimum income guarantee

There are new rates effective from 6 April 2003. — 88

CHAPTER 2

How much for you and how much for the tax inspector

A lmost everyone receives income that is liable to income tax in one form or another.

You may find, however, that you can avoid paying tax, or at least reduce your tax bill, by claiming personal allowances, by offsetting certain types of expenses or by changing where you invest your savings.

The allowances and expenses you can claim are dealt with later in this book. This chapter tells you what income is free from tax and what income is taxable.

Taxable income can be divided into two types: earned income and unearned, or investment, income.

The tax inspector can claim part of the following types of income

Earned income

Annuities from past jobs.

Benefits – private use of firm's car, petrol, services generally.

Benefits of cheap or interest-free loans from your employer for a non-qualifying purpose (see page 51).

Bereavement allowance.

Commission, including that from mail order companies, etc.

Compensation for loss of office (but see page 53).

Earnings from casual work and tips.

Expense allowances if not spent entirely on firm's business.

Holiday pay.

Incapacity benefit (except for the first 28 weeks).

Incentive schemes.

Income from furnished and unfurnished accommodation (but see page 60).

Income from overseas employment and pensions.

Income withdrawals from a delayed annuity pension plan.

Industrial death benefit if paid as a pension.

Invalid care allowance.

Jobseeker's allowance.

Luncheon vouchers – excess over 15p a day per person.
Pensions (from the State*, previous employers or your own scheme)
Profits from trades or professions.
Redundancy (see page 53).
Royalties earned from your own work.
Salaries, fees and bonuses.
Statutory maternity, paternity or adoption pay.
Statutory sick pay.
Stipends received by the clergy.
Wages.
Widowed parent's allowance.

*A married woman's retirement pension paid on the basis of her husband's contributions is treated as income of the wife.

Investment income

Annuities purchased.
Bank interest.
Building society interest.
Building society cash windfalls on a merger.
Dividends.
Gains from certain non-qualifying insurance policies.
Interest on National Savings Income Bonds and Capital Bonds.
Income from overseas investment and property.
Income from trusts and from estates of deceased persons.
National Savings Bank interest on investment accounts, but not the first £70 per person on ordinary accounts.
Rents and 'key' money (except holiday lettings) after expenses.
Reverse premiums.
Royalties – bought or inherited.
Stock or scrip dividends – dividends paid in shares instead of cash.

The various rates of tax are shown on page 139.

The following income is all yours – it is free of income tax

Adoption allowances under approved schemes.
Annuities resulting from gallantry awards.
Attendance allowance.
Awards for damages.
Bereavement payments.
Betting and pools winnings.
Car parking benefits.
Child benefit and allowances.
Child dependency additions paid with many State benefits.

Child tax credit and Children's tax credit.

Christmas bonus for pensioners from the State.

Compensation for loss of office, and redundancy pay up to £30,000 (but see page 53).

Compensation for mis-sold personal pensions and personal injury.

Disability or wounds pensions.

Disability living allowance.

Disabled person's tax credit (replaced by working tax credit).

Education grants and awards from a local authority or school.

Endowment policies.

Ex-gratia payments up to £30,000 (but see page 53).

Family income supplement and family credit.

Foster carer's income up to certain limits – for maximum amounts and details telephone 020 7438 6420.

Gifts for employees provided by third parties if under £150 a year (£250 from 2003-2004).

Gratuities from the armed forces.

Guardian's allowance.

Home improvement, repair and insulation grants.

Housing benefit and council tax benefit.

Incapacity benefit (if previously received as invalidity benefit at 12 April 1995 for the same incapacity and first 28 weeks of new claims).

Income support.

Individual savings accounts income (ISAs).

Industrial injury benefits.

Insurance policy benefits for accident, sickness, disability or unemployment from 6 April 1996 (earlier if mortgage linked).

Insurance bond withdrawals up to 5 per cent a year, but a portion may be subject to tax on redemption.

Interest from National Savings Certificates (including index-linked).

Interest on delayed tax repayments.

Invalidity pension.

Jobseeker's grant.

Life assurance policy bonuses and profits.

Long-service awards up to £20 for each year of service (but not cash). This is increased to £50 from 2003-2004.

Lottery winnings.

Lump sums from an approved pension scheme on retirement.

Luncheon vouchers up to 15p per person per day (any cash allowance would be taxable).

Maintenance or alimony (from 6 April 2000).

Maternity allowance.

Miners' coal allowance, whether in cash or kind.

National Savings Bank interest up to £70 per person on ordinary accounts only.

National Savings Certificates' increase in value.

One-parent benefit.

Pension tax credit.

Pensions from Austria or Germany to victims of Nazi persecution.

Personal equity plan dividends reinvested.

Premium Bond prizes.

Provident benefits up to £4,000 for lump sum payments.

Purchased life annuities – the capital proportion of yearly amount.

Rent and council tax rebates.

Rent-a-room relief up to £4,250 a year (see page 61).

SAYE schemes – interest and bonus.

Severe disablement allowances.

Shares issued under an approved share incentive scheme, authorised by a tax office, up to a value of £3,000 or, if greater, 10 per cent of the employee's earnings, subject to a maximum of £8,000. After five years the proceeds are tax free.

Share option profits made under the SAYE scheme run by the Department of National Savings – no income tax but capital gains tax may be payable.

Sickness benefits under an insurance policy for up to 12 months where the premiums are paid by the employee.

Social fund payments.

Statutory redundancy pay (see page 53).

Strike and unemployment pay from a trade union.

Student grants.

Subsidised or free bus travel to work.

Termination payments up to £30,000 (but see page 53).

TESSA interest if kept for the full period.

TOISA interest.

Training allowances.

Vaccine damage (lump sum).

Venture capital trust dividends (but see page 127).

War disablement pensions.

War widow's benefit.

Winter fuel payment for pensioners (there is a helpline – 0845 9151 515).

Working families' tax credit (up to 2002–2003).

Working tax credit (from 2003–2004).

CHAPTER 3

Tax forms and what to do with them

Tax return

You must fill in a tax return if the tax office send you one, or you are a higher-rate taxpayer, or if you are in partnership or self-employed, or you have income to declare on which tax is due. You will also want to fill in a tax return if you have paid too much tax and are due a refund.

If you need a tax return and haven't received one, then contact the tax office that deals with your employer's PAYE or, if you are self-employed or unemployed, then contact your local tax office.

There are time limits after which you will be charged penalties and interest (see page 46). Chapter 4 takes you step by step through all aspects of the tax return and any supplementary forms.

If you need supplementary tax return sheets, telephone the order line on 0845 9000 404.

There is a free Inland Revenue helpline on 0845 9000 444.

Notice of income tax code (form P2(T))

Don't just put this in a drawer! Check it as explained on page 78.

Make sure your employer knows of any alteration in your code, and write to your tax office if you disagree with any figure.

Form P60

Your employer has by law to give you this form by 31 May after the end of every tax year. It shows your earnings from that employment and the total PAYE deducted in the year.

Check the form to see if you can claim some tax back as shown on page 84.

Income tax repayment claim (form R40)

This will be sent to you by your tax office if most of your income has had tax deducted before receipt and you normally have to claim tax back at the end of each tax year.

There is a free Inland Revenue taxback helpline on 0845 0776 543.

Enquiry form (form 33)

This form is issued by the tax office covering your home address or a tax office that knows that you have been paid income by someone in their area. Complete and return it as soon as possible otherwise there could be delays in settling your tax matters in the future.

Notice of income paid gross (form RU6(M))

This is sent to people who have registered with banks or building societies to have their income paid gross – that is without having tax deducted.

Fill in the form carefully because the tax office send it to you to check your total income to make sure that you are not liable to pay tax (see page 92).

Notice of employee leaving (form P45)

This form is issued to you by your employer when you leave. If you are immediately going to another job, hand Parts 2 and 3 to your new employer. Otherwise, send them to the tax office shown on the form, together with a letter stating that you are at present unemployed, to see if you can claim a repayment of tax. Keep Part 1A, as this will help you to fill in your tax return.

If you do not have this form, or if you lose it, then you will have to complete a questionnaire form (P46) obtainable from your new employer. Your employer will send this to your tax office and use a temporary code until you either provide a P45 form or the tax office advises him of a new code for you.

Return of expenses and allowances (form P11D)

This is an annual form to be completed by an *employer* for staff who receive earnings, expenses and potential benefits of £8,500 a year or more, and for directors. It shows all perks, benefits and expenses that you were paid or given by your employer (see page 59).

There is also a form P9D for employees earning at a rate of less than £8,500 a year who have received benefits, etc. which are taxable.

Self assessment – tax calculation (form SA 302)

This notice summarises your income tax situation and shows how much is due or has been overpaid. You must check it carefully and ensure that the figures correspond to those stated in your tax return.

As well as setting out how your tax liability (or refund) is calculated, quite often there will be comments explaining certain figures or responding to queries you have raised.

It is easy to overlook these comments as the form is prepared on a computer and they don't stand out as they would in a conventional letter, therefore check the form carefully.

The calculation will not reflect any payments on account you may have made and you will therefore need to check the calculation with your statement of account (see below) to confirm your tax position.

If you cannot understand the calculations, or you have a query, telephone the Inland Revenue helpline on 0845 9000 444.

If you cannot submit your return because you have information outstanding, you should still estimate your tax liability and make payments by the due date to avoid interest and surcharges arising on any amount unpaid.

Self assessment – statement of account (form SA 300)

This statement, sent out by your tax office, shows how much tax is due and when it should be paid; it will also show, where applicable, any payments that are due on account.

If the statement shows you have paid too much tax and the overpayment has not been refunded to you, contact your tax office to request repayment.

One of the advantages of the self assessment tax system is that an individual now only deals with one tax office – in the past, particularly in the case of pensioners or those who have more than one employer, you could have been dealing with two or three tax offices.

General comments

You should not ignore any form or communication from the tax inspector but deal with it immediately, either by replying yourself or passing it on to the tax adviser who deals with your tax affairs.

The deadlines for returning your 2003 self assessment tax return are 30 September 2003 (or two months after the date the return form was sent to you, if later) if you want the tax inspector to calculate your tax liability or refund, or 31 January 2004 if you plan to do it yourself.

Interest and penalties for late submission of your tax return or tax payments are now very stringent (see page 46).

CHAPTER 4

How to fill in your 2003 tax return

Not everyone automatically receives a tax return to fill in every year, but if you do, you *must* complete it and return it to your tax office.

The tax office relies on the fact that it is the taxpayer's responsibility to advise them of any changes in sources of income or claims for expenses and allowances. You may, of course, ask for a tax return to complete if you do not receive one by telephoning your local tax office or the tax office that deals with your PAYE if you are employed.

A husband and wife are treated as individuals in their own right for tax purposes, getting their own tax return, being responsible for their own tax affairs and getting their own individual tax allowances and exemptions.

The tax year runs from 6 April in one year to 5 April in the following year.

Your tax return for the year ended 5 April 2003 is a ten-page document with dozens of boxes for you to complete; it summarises your income and reliefs and enables you to claim allowances for that year.

Start filling in your tax return by ticking the appropriate boxes on page 2 (reproduced overleaf).

If you answer yes to any of the questions numbered 1 to 9, then check to see if the tax office have sent you the relevant supplementary pages to complete. If not, then telephone the special order line on 0845 9000 404 and ask for the required pages. You will need to quote your name, address and tax reference number. Alternatively, you can fax on 0845 9000 604 or download the forms from the Inland Revenue website www.inlandrevenue.gov.uk/sa.

Blind persons requiring help with a Braille version should contact their local tax office.

The tax return and all the supplementary pages are now reproduced in this book, starting on the next page.

Overview and supplementary pages

To summarise the steps you need to take:

1. Read the questions on page 2 of the main tax return (reproduced below) and tick the 'Yes' boxes where they apply to you.
2. Make sure you have all the supplementary pages that you need (as listed opposite).
3. Fill in the supplementary pages corresponding to the 'Yes' boxes.
4. Fill in the rest of the boxes in the main tax return.

INCOME AND CAPITAL GAINS *for the year ended 5 April 2003*

Step 1

Answer Questions 1 to 9 below to check if you need supplementary Pages to give details of particular income or capital gains. Pages 6 and 7 of your Tax Return Guide will help.

(Ask the Orderline for a Guide if I haven't sent you one with your Tax Return, and you want one.)

If you answer 'Yes' ask the Orderline for the appropriate supplementary Pages and Notes.

Ring the Orderline on 0845 9000 404, or fax on 0845 9000 604 for any you need (closed Christmas Day, Boxing Day and New Year's Day).

If you do need supplementary Pages, tick the boxes below when you've got them.

Q1 Were you an employee, or office holder, or director, or agency worker or did you receive payments or benefits from a former employer (excluding a pension) in the year ended 5 April 2003?
If you were a non-resident director of a UK company but received no remuneration, see the notes to the Employment Pages, page EN3, box 1.6.

YES [ ]   EMPLOYMENT [ ]

Q2 Did you have any taxable income from share options, shares or share related benefits in the year? (This does not include
- dividends, **or**
- dividend shares ceasing to be subject to an Inland Revenue approved share incentive plan within three years of acquisition they go in Question 10.)

YES [ ]   SHARE SCHEMES [ ]

Q3 Were you self-employed (but not in partnership)?
(You should also tick 'Yes' if you were a Name at Lloyd's.)

YES [ ]   SELF-EMPLOYMENT [ ]

Q4 Were you in partnership?

YES [ ]   PARTNERSHIP [ ]

Q5 Did you receive any rent or other income from land and property in the year?

YES [ ]   LAND & PROPERTY [ ]

Q6 Did you have any taxable income from overseas pensions or benefits, or from foreign companies or savings institutions, offshore funds or trusts abroad, or from land and property abroad or gains on foreign insurance policies?

YES [ ]

Have you or could you have received, or enjoyed directly or indirectly, or benefited in any way from, income of a foreign entity as a result of a transfer of assets made in this or earlier years?

YES [ ]

Do you want to claim foreign tax credit relief for foreign tax paid on foreign income or gains?

YES [ ]   FOREIGN [ ]

Q7 Did you receive, or are you deemed to have, income from a trust, settlement or the residue of a deceased person's estate?

YES [ ]   TRUSTS ETC [ ]

Q8 Capital gains - read the guidance on page 7 of the Tax Return Guide.
- If you have disposed of your only or main residence do you need the Capital Gains Pages?

YES [ ]

- Did you dispose of other chargeable assets worth more than £15,400 in total?

YES [ ]

- Were your total chargeable gains more than £7,700 or do you want to make a claim or election for the year?

YES [ ]   CAPITAL GAINS [ ]

Q9 Are you claiming that you were not resident, or not ordinarily resident, or not domiciled, in the UK, or dual resident in the UK and another country, for all or part of the year?

YES [ ]   NON-RESIDENCE ETC [ ]

Step 2 **Fill in any supplementary Pages BEFORE going to Step 3.**
Please use blue or black ink to fill in your Tax Return and please do not include pence. Round down your income and gains. Round up your tax credits and tax deductions. Round to the nearest pound.
When you have filled in all the supplementary Pages you need, tick this box. [ ]

Step 3 Fill in Questions 10 to 24. If you answer 'Yes', fill in the relevant boxes. If not applicable, go to the next question.

Supplementary pages

Employment

The supplementary pages headed Employment cover your income and benefits from employment and your claim for expenses. (There are different versions of this form for Ministers of Religion and Members of Parliament.)

After each section there is a cross-reference to the chapter or page in this book that will give you help in filling in this form.

To fill in these sections you may need copies of your:

P60 or P45 forms	
Notice of tax code	
P11D form	
Receipts for expenses, etc.	

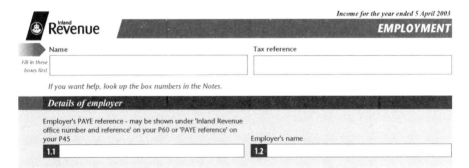

Box **1.1** Your employer's PAYE reference should be on your P60 or P45 form.

Date employment started
(only if between 6 April 2002 and 5 April 2003)

1.3 /   /

Date employment finished
(only if between 6 April 2002 and 5 April 2003)

1.4 /   /

Tick box 1.6 if you were
a director of the company

1.6

and, if so, tick box 1.7
if it was a close company

1.7

Employer's address

1.5

Postcode

Income from employment

■ **Money** - see Notes, page EN3

- Payments from P60 (or P45)

Before tax

1.8 £

- Payments not on P60 etc.   - tips

1.9 £

- other payments (excluding expenses entered below and lump sums
and compensation payments or benefits entered overleaf)

1.10 £

Tax deducted

- **Tax deducted** in the UK from payments in boxes 1.8 to 1.10

1.11 £

Boxes **1.8** to **1.11** see page 47. You *are* allowed to subtract any deduction made by your employer for your contributions to an approved pension scheme, payroll giving donations, or lump sum leaving payment.

■ **Benefits and expenses** - see Notes, pages EN3 to EN6. If any benefits connected with termination of employment were received, or enjoyed, after that termination and were from a **former** employer you need to complete Help Sheet IR204, available from the Orderline. Do not enter such benefits here.

- Assets transferred/
payments made for you

Amount

1.12 £

- Vans

Amount

1.18 £

- Vouchers, credit cards
and tokens

Amount

1.13 £

- Interest-free and low-interest loans
see Note for box 1.19, page EN5

Amount

1.19 £

- Living accommodation

Amount

1.14 £

box 1.20 is not used

- Excess mileage allowances
and passenger payments

Amount

1.15 £

- Private medical or
dental insurance

Amount

1.21 £

- Company cars

Amount

1.16 £

- Other benefits

Amount

1.22 £

- Fuel for company cars

Amount

1.17 £

- Expenses payments received
and balancing charges

Amount

1.23 £

Box no. **1.12** see page 52.   Box no. **1.15** see page 50.

Box no. **1.13** see page 52.   Box no. **1.16** see page 48.

Box no. **1.14** see page 51.   Box no. **1.17** see page 50.

continued overleaf

Box no. **1.18** see page 50.   Box no. **1.22** see page 51.

Box no. **1.19** see page 51.   Box no. **1.23** see pages 54 and 103.

Box no. **1.21** see page 52.

Income from employment continued

■ *Lump sums and compensation payments or benefits including such payments and benefits from a former employer*
Note that 'lump sums' here includes any contributions which your employer made to an unapproved retirement benefits scheme

*You must read page EN6 of the Notes **before** filling in boxes 1.24 to 1.30*

Reliefs

- £30,000 exemption — **1.24** £
- Foreign service and disability — **1.25** £
- Retirement and death lump sums — **1.26** £

Taxable lump sums

- From box B of *Help Sheet IR204* — **1.27** £
- From box K of *Help Sheet IR204* — **1.28** £
- From box L of *Help Sheet IR204* — **1.29** £
- Tax deducted from payments in boxes 1.27 to 1.29 - *leave blank if this tax is included in the box 1.11 figure.* Tax deducted **1.30** £

Boxes **1.24** to **1.30** see page 53.

■ *Foreign earnings not taxable in the UK in the year ended 5 April 2003* - see Notes, page EN6 **1.31** £

■ *Expenses you incurred in doing your job* - see Notes, pages EN7 to EN8

- Travel and subsistence costs **1.32** £
- Fixed deductions for expenses **1.33** £
- Professional fees and subscriptions **1.34** £
- Other expenses and capital allowances **1.35** £
- Tick box 1.36 if the figure in box 1.32 includes travel between your home and a permanent workplace **1.36**

■ *Foreign Earnings Deduction* (seafarers only) **1.37** £

■ *Foreign tax for which tax credit relief not claimed* **1.38** £

Box no. **1.31** see page 55.   Box no. **1.35** see pages 57 and 103.

Box no. **1.32** see page 58.   Box no. **1.36** see page 58.

Box no. **1.33** see page 57.   Box no. **1.37** see page 55.

Box no. **1.34** see page 58.   Box no. **1.38** see page 55.

Where there are several figures to go in one box, use a separate sheet to add them together and keep a copy to which you can refer at any time.

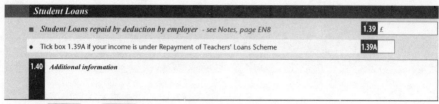

Boxes **1.39** to **1.40** see page 74.

Share schemes

The supplementary pages headed Share schemes cover share options and share-related benefits.

To fill in these sections you may need copies of:

Share option certificates	
Correspondence from your scheme's trustees	
Market valuations at relevant dates	

You must complete a separate page for each share scheme – you cannot group them together. Telephone the order line on 0845 9000 404 if you want another form. Help sheet IR218 is also available from that number.

As the rules and regulations vary from scheme to scheme, consult your employer or the trustees of your scheme if you require help or advice before filling in your tax return.

General background information on share schemes is given on page 54.

These supplementary pages only cover any liability to income tax; if you have made any capital gains or losses on disposing of the shares, you may need to declare these in the Capital gains supplementary pages (see pages 33 and 110).

Inland Revenue

Income for the year ended 5 April 2003

SHARE SCHEMES

Fill in these boxes first

Name

Tax reference

If you want help, look up the box numbers in the Notes.

Share options

Read the Notes on pages SN1 to SN8 before filling in the boxes

■ *Approved savings-related share options*

		Name of company and share scheme	Tick if shares unlisted	Taxable amount
● Exercise	2.1		2.2	2.3 £
● Cancellation or release	2.4		2.5	2.6 £

■ *Approved discretionary share options*

Name of company and share scheme

● Exercise | 2.7 | 2.8 | 2.9 £

● Cancellation or release | 2.10 | 2.11 | 2.12 £

■ *Enterprise Management Incentive options*

Name of company and unique option reference

● Exercise | 2.13 | 2.14 | 2.15 £

● Cancellation or release | 2.16 | 2.17 | 2.18 £

■ *Unapproved share options*

Name of company and share scheme

● Grant | 2.19 | 2.20 | 2.21 £

● Exercise | 2.22 | 2.23 | 2.24 £

● Cancellation or release | 2.25 | 2.26 | 2.27 £

Continue filling this column, as appropriate, and make sure you fill in boxes 2.40 and 2.42

Approved Share Incentive Plans

Read the Notes on page SN2 **before** filling in the boxes

Name of company and share plan

● Shares ceasing to be subject to the plan | 2.28 | 2.29 | 2.30 £

Shares acquired

Read the Notes on page SN8 **before** filling in the boxes

Name of company and share scheme

● Shares acquired from your employment | 2.31 | 2.32 | 2.33 £

● Shares as benefits | 2.34 | 2.35 | 2.36 £

● Post-acquisition charges or lifting of risk of forfeiture | 2.37 | 2.38 | 2.39 £

■ *Totals*

● Total of the taxable amounts boxes (total boxes in the right-hand column, starting with box 2.3)

total column above
2.40 £

● Any taxable amounts included in boxes 2.6 to 2.39 which are included in the Pay figure on your P60 or P45(Part 1A)

2.41 £

Total taxable amount

box 2.40 *minus* box 2.41
2.42 £

Share options

Read the Notes on pages SN2 to SN8 **before** filling in the boxes

Name of company and share scheme

2.43 | Class of share (for example, 10p Ordinary)
2.44

	Options granted	Options exercised	Options cancelled/released
2.45 Date option was granted	/ /	/ /	/ /
2.46 Date option was exercised		/ /	
2.47 Number of shares			
2.48 Exercise price: option price per share	£ .	£ .	
2.49 Amount, if any, paid for grant of option	£ .	£ .	£ .
2.50 Market value per share at date the option was granted	£ .		
2.51 Market value per share at date the option was exercised		£ .	
2.52 Amount received in money or money's worth			£ .

Enterprise Management Incentive options

*Read the Notes on pages SN3 to SN6 **before** filling in the boxes*

Name of company and unique option reference

2.53 [   ] **2.54** Class of share (for example, 10p Ordinary) [   ]

		Options exercised	Options cancelled/released
2.55	Date option was granted	/ /	/ /
2.56	Date of disqualifying event	/ /	
2.57	Number of shares		
2.58	Exercise price: option price per share	£ .	
2.59	Amount, if any, paid for grant of option	£ .	£ .
2.60	Market value per share at date the option was granted	£ .	
2.61	Market value per share at date of the disqualifying event	£ .	
2.62	Market value per share at date the option was exercised	£ .	
2.63	Amount received in money or money's worth		£ .

Approved Share Incentive Plans

*Read the Notes on page SN2 **before** filling in the boxes*

Name of company and share plan

2.64 [   ] **2.65** Class of shares (for example 10p Ordinary) [   ]

2.66	Date shares ceased to be subject to the plan	/ /
2.67	Market value per share when shares ceased to be subject to the plan	£ .
2.68	Number of shares	

Shares acquired

*Read the Notes on page SN8 **before** filling in the boxes*

Name of company and share scheme

2.69 [   ] **2.70** Class of share (for example, 10p Ordinary) [   ]

		Shares acquired	Post-acquisition charge
2.71	Date shares acquired or forfeiture lifted	/ /	/ /
2.72	Number of shares		
2.73	Amount paid per share	£ .	
2.74	Market value per share at date of acquisition or forfeiture lifted	£ .	£ .
2.75	Give details of the nature of the post-acquisition event		

Income Tax paid

- Income Tax paid on the grant of your option **2.76** £

2.77 *Additional information*

Self-employment

The supplementary pages headed Self-employment cover your business details and a separate sheet needs to be completed for each business. You must fill in these pages if you received income from work done on a self-employed or freelance basis, or you let furnished rooms and provided services so that it was considered as a business – but not if you were in partnership. If you were in partnership, you need the Partnership supplementary pages (see page 27). There is a different version for Lloyd's Underwriting Names.

If your turnover is less than £15,000 a year, you do not need to fill in Boxes 3.27 to 3.73 of this form.

Although these supplementary pages appear very complicated at first glance, they are basically requesting the information that should be available from your business accounts but broken down under individual boxes for turnover and expense headings, with separate boxes for capital allowances, adjustments to profits for tax purposes and carrying forward of any losses.

Chapter 14 in this book covers all basic aspects of self-employment.

Inland Revenue

Income for the year ended 5 April 2003

SELF-EMPLOYMENT

Fill in these boxes first

Name	Tax reference

If you want help, look up the box numbers in the Notes

Business details

Name of business
3.1

Description of business
3.2

Address of business
3.3

Postcode

Accounting period - *read the Notes, page SEN2 before filling in these boxes*

Start	End
3.4 / /	**3.5** / /

- Tick box 3.6 if details in boxes 3.1 or 3.3 have changed since your last Tax Return **3.6**

- Date of commencement if after 5 April 2000 **3.7** / /

- Date of cessation if before 6 April 2003 **3.8** / /

- Tick box 3.9 if the special arrangements for certain trades apply - *read the Notes, pages SEN11 and SEN12* **3.9**

- Tick box 3.10 if you entered details for all relevant accounting periods on last year's Tax Return and boxes 3.14 to 3.73 and 3.99 to 3.115 will be blank (*read Step 3 on page SEN2*) **3.10**

- Tick box 3.11 if your accounts do not cover the period from the last accounting date (explain why in the 'Additional information' box, box 3.116) **3.11**

- Tick box 3.12 if your accounting date has changed (only if this is a permanent change and you want it to count for tax) **3.12**

- Tick box 3.13 if this is the second or further change (explain in box 3.116 on Page SE4 why you have not used the same date as last year) **3.13**

Boxes **3.11** to **3.13** see page 97.

Capital allowances - summary

	Capital allowances	Balancing charges
• Cars costing more than £12,000 (a separate calculation must be made for each car.)	3.14 £	3.15 £
• Other business plant and machinery	3.16 £	3.17 £
• Agricultural or Industrial Buildings Allowance (A separate calculation must be made for each block of expenditure.)	3.18 £	3.19 £
• Other capital allowances claimed (Separate calculations must be made.)	3.20 £	3.21 £
	total of column above	total of column above
Total capital allowances/balancing charges	3.22 £	3.23 £
• Tick box 3.22A if box 3.22 includes enhanced capital allowances for environmentally friendly expenditure	3.22A	

Income and expenses - annual turnover below £15,000

If your annual turnover is £15,000 or more, ignore boxes 3.24 to 3.26. Instead fill in Page SE2

If your annual turnover is below £15,000, fill in boxes 3.24 to 3.26 instead of Page SE2. Read the Notes, page SEN2.

• Turnover including other business receipts and goods etc. taken for personal use (and balancing charges from box 3.23)	3.24 £
• Expenses allowable for tax (including capital allowances from box 3.22)	3.25 £
	box 3.24 minus box 3.25
Net profit (put figure in brackets if a loss)	3.26 £

Boxes **3.14** to **3.23** see page 103.

Boxes **3.24** to **3.26** see page 101.

Income and expenses - annual turnover £15,000 or more

You must fill in this Page if your annual turnover is £15,000 or more - read the Notes, page SEN2

If you were registered for VAT, do the figures in boxes 3.29 to 3.64, include VAT? 3.27   or exclude VAT? 3.28   Sales/business income (turnover) 3.29 £

	Disallowable expenses included in boxes 3.46 to 3.63	Total expenses	
• Cost of sales	3.30 £	3.46 £	
• Construction industry subcontractor costs	3.31 £	3.47 £	
• Other direct costs	3.32 £	3.48 £	
			box 3.29 minus (boxes 3.46 + 3.47 + 3.48)
		Gross profit/(loss)	3.49 £
		Other income/profits	3.50 £
• Employee costs	3.33 £	3.51 £	
• Premises costs	3.34 £	3.52 £	
• Repairs	3.35 £	3.53 £	
• General administrative expenses	3.36 £	3.54 £	
• Motor expenses	3.37 £	3.55 £	
• Travel and subsistence	3.38 £	3.56 £	
• Advertising, promotion and entertainment	3.39 £	3.57 £	
• Legal and professional costs	3.40 £	3.58 £	
• Bad debts	3.41 £	3.59 £	
• Interest	3.42 £	3.60 £	
• Other finance charges	3.43 £	3.61 £	
• Depreciation and loss/(profit) on sale	3.44 £	3.62 £	

● Other expenses	**3.45** £ Put the total of boxes 3.30 to 3.45 in box 3.66 below	**3.63** £	total of boxes 3.51 to 3.63
		Total expenses	**3.64** £
			boxes 3.49 + 3.50 *minus* 3.64
		Net profit/(loss)	**3.65** £

Tax adjustments to net profit or loss

		boxes 3.30 to 3.45
● Disallowable expenses	**3.66** £	
● Adjustments (apart from disallowable expenses) that increase profits. Examples are goods taken for personal use and amounts brought forward from an earlier year because of a claim under ESC B11 about compulsory slaughter of farm animals	**3.67** £	
● Balancing charges (from box 3.23)	**3.68** £	
		boxes 3.66 + 3.67 + 3.68
Total additions to net profit (deduct from net loss)		**3.69** £
● Capital allowances (from box 3.22)	**3.70** £	
		boxes 3.70 + 3.71
● Deductions from net profit (add to net loss)	**3.71** £	**3.72** £
		boxes 3.65 + 3.69 *minus* 3.72
Net business profit for tax purposes (put figure in brackets if a loss)		**3.73** £

Boxes **3.27** to **3.73** see page 100.

Adjustments to arrive at taxable profit or loss

Basis period begins	**3.74** / /	and ends	**3.75** / /

Profit or loss of this account for tax purposes (box 3.26 or 3.73)	**3.76** £
Adjustment to arrive at profit or loss for this basis period	**3.77** £

● Overlap profit brought forward	**3.78** £	● Deduct overlap relief used this year **3.79** £
● Overlap profit carried forward	**3.80** £	

Averaging for farmers and creators of literary or artistic works *(see Notes, page SEN9, if you made a loss for 2002-03)*	**3.81** £
Adjustment on change of basis	**3.82** £
Net profit for 2002-03 (if you made a loss, enter '0')	**3.83** £

Allowable loss for 2002-03 (if you made a profit, enter '0')	**3.84** £	
● Loss offset against other income for 2002-03	**3.85** £	
● Loss to carry back	**3.86** £	
● Loss to carry forward (that is allowable loss not claimed in any other way)	**3.87** £	
● Losses brought forward from earlier years	**3.88** £	
● Losses brought forward from earlier years used this year		**3.89** £
		box 3.83 *minus* box 3.89
Taxable profit after losses brought forward		**3.90** £
● Any other business income (for example, Business Start-up Allowance received in 2002-03)		**3.91** £
		box 3.90 + box 3.91
Total taxable profits from this business		**3.92** £
● Tick box 3.93 if the figure in box 3.92 is provisional		**3.93**

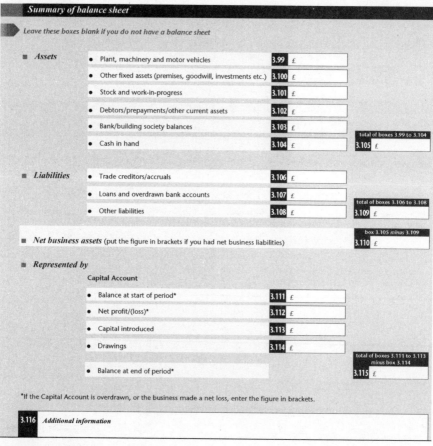

Class 4 National Insurance contributions

- Tick box 3.94 if exception or deferment applies — 3.94
- Adjustments to profit chargeable to Class 4 National Insurance contributions — 3.95 £
- Class 4 National Insurance contributions due — 3.96 £

Subcontractors in the construction industry

- Deductions made by contractors on account of tax (please send your CIS25s to us) — 3.97 £

Tax deducted from trading income

- Any tax deducted (excluding deductions made by contractors on account of tax) from trading income — 3.98 £

Boxes **3.74** to **3.98** see page 104.

Summary of balance sheet

Leave these boxes blank if you do not have a balance sheet

■ **Assets**
- Plant, machinery and motor vehicles — 3.99 £
- Other fixed assets (premises, goodwill, investments etc.) — 3.100 £
- Stock and work-in-progress — 3.101 £
- Debtors/prepayments/other current assets — 3.102 £
- Bank/building society balances — 3.103 £
- Cash in hand — 3.104 £   total of boxes 3.99 to 3.104 — 3.105 £

■ **Liabilities**
- Trade creditors/accruals — 3.106 £
- Loans and overdrawn bank accounts — 3.107 £
- Other liabilities — 3.108 £   total of boxes 3.106 to 3.108 — 3.109 £

■ **Net business assets** (put the figure in brackets if you had net business liabilities)   box 3.105 minus 3.109 — 3.110 £

■ **Represented by**

Capital Account
- Balance at start of period* — 3.111 £
- Net profit/(loss)* — 3.112 £
- Capital introduced — 3.113 £
- Drawings — 3.114 £
- Balance at end of period*   total of boxes 3.111 to 3.113 minus box 3.114 — 3.115 £

*If the Capital Account is overdrawn, or the business made a net loss, enter the figure in brackets.

3.116   *Additional information*

Partnership

The Partnership supplementary pages are not reproduced here in full, as the background information needed to complete them is similar to that covered by the Self-employment section (see page 23) and Chapter 14 covers most of the basic aspects.

There are two types of supplementary pages: Partnership (short) reproduced here and Partnership (full). Use the short version if your only partnership income was trading income or taxed interest from banks, building societies and deposit takers. This will apply to the majority of small partnerships.

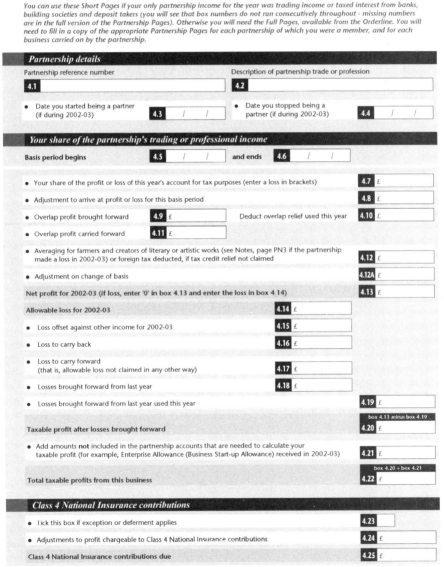

Income for the year ended 5 April 2003

Inland Revenue

PARTNERSHIP (SHORT)

If you have answered 'Yes' to Question 4, fill in Pages P1 and P2. If you want help, look up the box number in the Notes on Partnership. These will be at the back of your Tax Return Guide, if I've sent you one, or you can get them from the Orderline or our website. The Notes are colour-coded to match this form.

You can use these Short Pages if your only partnership income for the year was trading income or taxed interest from banks, building societies and deposit takers (you will see that box numbers do not run consecutively throughout - missing numbers are in the full version of the Partnership Pages). Otherwise you will need the Full Pages, available from the Orderline. You will need to fill in a copy of the appropriate Partnership Pages for each partnership of which you were a member, and for each business carried on by the partnership.

Partnership details

Partnership reference number — 4.1

Description of partnership trade or profession — 4.2

- Date you started being a partner (if during 2002-03) — 4.3 / /
- Date you stopped being a partner (if during 2002-03) — 4.4 / /

Your share of the partnership's trading or professional income

Basis period begins — 4.5 / / and ends — 4.6 / /

- Your share of the profit or loss of this year's account for tax purposes (enter a loss in brackets) — 4.7 £
- Adjustment to arrive at profit or loss for this basis period — 4.8 £
- Overlap profit brought forward — 4.9 £   Deduct overlap relief used this year — 4.10 £
- Overlap profit carried forward — 4.11 £
- Averaging for farmers and creators of literary or artistic works (see Notes, page PN3 if the partnership made a loss in 2002-03) or foreign tax deducted, if tax credit relief not claimed — 4.12 £
- Adjustment on change of basis — 4.12A £

Net profit for 2002-03 (if loss, enter '0' in box 4.13 and enter the loss in box 4.14) — 4.13 £

Allowable loss for 2002-03 — 4.14 £

- Loss offset against other income for 2002-03 — 4.15 £
- Loss to carry back — 4.16 £
- Loss to carry forward (that is, allowable loss not claimed in any other way) — 4.17 £
- Losses brought forward from last year — 4.18 £
- Losses brought forward from last year used this year — 4.19 £

Taxable profit after losses brought forward — box 4.13 *minus* box 4.19 — 4.20 £

- Add amounts **not** included in the partnership accounts that are needed to calculate your taxable profit (for example, Enterprise Allowance (Business Start-up Allowance) received in 2002-03) — 4.21 £

Total taxable profits from this business — box 4.20 + box 4.21 — 4.22 £

Class 4 National Insurance contributions

- Tick this box if exception or deferment applies — 4.23
- Adjustments to profit chargeable to Class 4 National Insurance contributions — 4.24 £

Class 4 National Insurance contributions due — 4.25 £

Refer to Chapter 15 for the National Insurance implications.

Your share of the partnership taxed income

- Share of taxed income (liable at 20%) **4.70** £

Your share of the partnership trading and professional profits

from box 4.22

- Share of partnership profits (other than that liable at 20%) **4.73** £

Your share of the partnership tax paid

- Share of Income Tax deducted from partnership income **4.74** £
- Share of CIS25 deductions **4.75** £
- Share of tax deducted from trading income (not CIS25 deductions) **4.75A** £

boxes 4.74 + 4.75 + 4.75A

4.77 £

4.79 *Additional information*

Land and Property

The supplementary pages headed Land and property cover all types of UK rental income, whether it is from numerous properties or a single rental, holiday lettings or qualifies for a Rent-a-room relief. (Any income from land or property overseas should not be included here – ask for the Foreign supplementary pages.)

Pages 60–61 give you background details to the taxation of land and buildings, joint holdings and expenses payments that you might be able to claim.

If you are only claiming Rent-a-room relief (see page 61) you need to tick the 'Yes' box. There is no need to fill in any other section.

To fill in these sections of the tax return you will need:

Records of rent received	
Records of expenses and bills for them	

Inland **Revenue**

Income for the year ended 5 April 2003

LAND AND PROPERTY

Name

Tax reference

Fill in these boxes first

If you want help, look up the box numbers in the Notes.

Are you claiming Rent a Room relief for gross rents of £4,250 or less?
(Or £2,125 if the claim is shared?)
Read the Notes on page LN2 to find out
- whether you can claim Rent a Room relief; and
- how to claim relief for gross rents over £4,250

Yes

If 'Yes', tick box. If this is your only income from UK property, you have finished these Pages

Is your income from furnished holiday lettings?
If not applicable, please turn over and fill in Page L2 to give details of your property income

Yes

If 'Yes', tick box and fill in boxes 5.1 to 5.18 before completing Page L2

Furnished holiday lettings

- Income from furnished holiday lettings **5.1** £

Expenses (furnished holiday lettings only)

- Rent, rates, insurance, ground rents etc. **5.2** £
- Repairs, maintenance and renewals **5.3** £
- Finance charges, including interest **5.4** £
- Legal and professional costs **5.5** f
- Costs of services provided, including wages **5.6** £
- Other expenses **5.7** £

total of boxes 5.2 to 5.7
5.8 £

Net profit (put figures in brackets if a loss)

box 5.1 *minus* box 5.8
5.9 £

Tax adjustments

- Private use **5.10** £
- Balancing charges **5.11** £

box 5.10 + box 5.11
5.12 £

- Capital allowances **5.13** £

- Tick box 5.13A if box 5.13 includes enhanced capital allowances for environmentally friendly expenditure **5.13A**

Profit for the year (copy to box 5.19). If loss, enter '0' in box 5.14 and put the loss in box 5.15

boxes 5.9 + 5.12 *minus* box 5.13
5.14 £

Loss for the year (if you have entered '0' in box 5.14)

boxes 5.9 + 5.12 *minus* box 5.13
5.15 £

Losses

- Loss offset against 2002-03 total income **5.16** £

see Notes, page LN4
- Loss carried back **5.17** £

see Notes, page LN4
- Loss offset against other income from property (copy to box 5.38) **5.18** £

Other property income

Income

- Furnished holiday lettings profits

copy from box 5.14
5.19 £

- Rents and other income from land and property **5.20** £

Tax deducted
5.21 £

- Chargeable premiums **5.22** £
- Reverse premiums **5.22A** £

boxes 5.19 + 5.20 + 5.22 + 5.22A
5.23 £

Expenses (do not include figures you have already put in boxes 5.2 to 5.7 on Page L1)

- Rent, rates, insurance, ground rents etc. **5.24** £
- Repairs, maintenance and renewals **5.25** £
- Finance charges, including interest **5.26** £
- Legal and professional costs **5.27** £
- Costs of services provided, including wages **5.28** £
- Other expenses **5.29** f

total of boxes 5.24 to 5.29
5.30 £

Net profit (put figures in brackets if a loss)

box 5.23 *minus* box 5.30
5.31 £

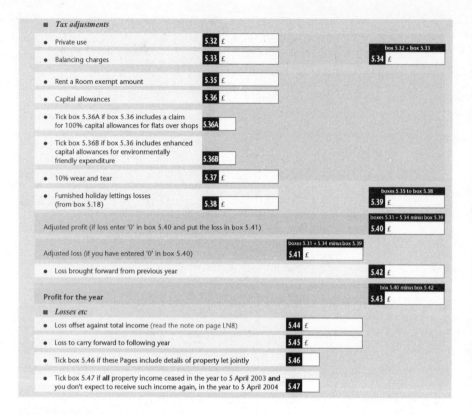

- **Tax adjustments**

- Private use — 5.32 £
- Balancing charges — 5.33 £
  - box 5.32 + box 5.33 — 5.34 £
- Rent a Room exempt amount — 5.35 £
- Capital allowances — 5.36 £
- Tick box 5.36A if box 5.36 includes a claim for 100% capital allowances for flats over shops — 5.36A
- Tick box 5.36B if box 5.36 includes enhanced capital allowances for environmentally friendly expenditure — 5.36B
- 10% wear and tear — 5.37 £
- Furnished holiday lettings losses (from box 5.18) — 5.38 £
  - boxes 5.35 to box 5.38 — 5.39 £

Adjusted profit (if loss enter '0' in box 5.40 and put the loss in box 5.41) — boxes 5.31 + 5.34 *minus* box 5.39 — 5.40 £

Adjusted loss (if you have entered '0' in box 5.40) — boxes 5.31 + 5.34 *minus* box 5.39 — 5.41 £

- Loss brought forward from previous year — 5.42 £

Profit for the year — box 5.40 *minus* box 5.42 — 5.43 £

- **Losses etc**

- Loss offset against total income (read the note on page LN8) — 5.44 £
- Loss to carry forward to following year — 5.45 £
- Tick box 5.46 if these Pages include details of property let jointly — 5.46
- Tick box 5.47 if **all** property income ceased in the year to 5 April 2003 **and** you don't expect to receive such income again, in the year to 5 April 2004 — 5.47

Foreign

The supplementary pages headed Foreign cover all income, pensions and benefits that you receive from abroad.

These pages only apply to *income* from abroad. If you have made capital gains or losses, then these should be declared on the Capital gains supplementary pages, although any foreign tax incurred should be stated here.

Inland Revenue

Income and gains and foreign tax credit relief for the year ended 5 April 2003

FOREIGN

Fill in these boxes first

Name

Tax reference

Foreign savings

Fill in columns A, B, D and E, and tick the box in column E if you want to claim foreign tax credit relief.

Country A	tick box if income is unremittable	Amount before tax B	Foreign tax D	Amount chargeable E tick box to claim foreign tax credit relief
				total of column above 6.1 £
				total of column above 6.2 £

Foreign savings income taxable on the remittance basis and foreign income from overseas pensions or social security benefits, from land and property abroad, chargeable premiums or income/benefits received from overseas trusts, companies and other entities

total of column above	total of column above
6.3 £	6.4 £

total of column above	total of column above
6.3A £	6.4A £

- Disposals of holdings in offshore funds, income from non-resident trusts and benefits received from overseas trusts, companies and other entities - *see Notes, page FN11.*   **6.5** £

  Tick box 6.5A if you are omitting income from boxes 6.4, 6.4A or 6.5 - *see Notes, pages FN11 and FN12.*   **6.5A**

- Gains on foreign life insurance policies etc. - *see Notes page FN12.*

Number of years	Tax treated as paid	Gains(s)
6.6	6.7 £	6.8 £

- If you are calculating your tax, enter the total foreign tax credit relief on your income in box 6.9 - *see Notes, pages FN15 and FN16.*   **6.9** £

- If you are calculating your tax, enter the total foreign tax credit relief on your gains in box 6.10 - *see Notes, page FN15.*   **6.10** £

Boxes **6.11** to **6.25** cover your expenditure headings (these are not reproduced here).

	box 6.19 + box 6.22 minus box 6.25
Adjusted profit (if loss, enter '0' here, and enter loss in box 6.27)	6.26 £

	box 6.19 + box 6.22 minus box 6.25
Adjusted loss (if you have entered '0' in box 6.26)	6.27 £

Income from land and property abroad, continued

Fill in boxes 6.28 to 6.32 (if you have completed only one Page F4) **or** boxes 6.33 to 6.38 if you have completed a separate Page F4 for each property.

- Taxable profit or allowable loss from box 6.26 or 6.27 (enter a loss in brackets)   **6.28** £

  minus losses brought forward from earlier years   **6.29** £

  Total taxable profits (if box 6.28 is a profit and is more than box 6.29)   **6.30** £   *box 6.28 minus 6.29*
  Copy to column B on Page F2

  or loss to carry forward (if box 6.28 is a profit but less than box 6.29, enter box 6.29 *minus* box 6.28, or, if box 6.28 is a loss, enter box 6.28 *plus* box 6.29)   **6.31** £

- If you have only one property or your properties are all in the same foreign country and foreign tax was deducted, enter the tax paid   **6.32** £

total column above		
6.33 £		

minus losses brought forward from earlier years   **6.34** £

Total taxable profits		
6.35 £	6.36 £	6.37 £
Copy to column B on Page F2	*Copy to column D on Page F2*	*Copy to column E on Page F2*

or loss to carry forward   **6.38** £

6.39   *Additional information*

Trusts etc.

The supplementary pages headed Trusts etc. enable you to declare any income you receive from trusts, settlements or estates of deceased persons. Tax deducted from such income may be at different tax rates, and you need to identify these in the boxes.

To fill in these sections you will need:

Dividend and interest statements from the trustees or personal representatives	
Correspondence identifying the type of trust, etc.	

See also page 62 for further background information.

Inland Revenue

Income for the year ended 5 April 2003

TRUSTS ETC.

Fill in these boxes first

Name

Tax reference

If you want help, look up the box numbers in the Notes

Income from trusts and settlements

■ *Income taxed at:*

	Income receivable	Tax paid	
the 'rate applicable to trusts'	7.1 £	7.2 £	7.3 £
the basic rate	7.4 £	7.5 £	7.6 £
the lower rate	7.7 £	7.8 £	7.9 £
the dividend rate	7.10 £	7.11 £	7.12 £

Tick this box if you have included in your Tax Return, income from trusts or settlements whose trustees are not resident in the UK for tax purposes   7.12A

Income from the estates of deceased persons

■ *Income bearing:*

	Income receivable	Tax paid	Taxable amount
basic rate tax	7.13 £	7.14 £	7.15 £
lower rate tax	7.16 £	7.17 £	7.18 £
repayable dividend rate	7.19 £	7.20 £	7.21 £
non-repayable basic rate tax	7.22 £	7.23 £	7.24 £
non-repayable lower rate tax	7.25 £	7.26 £	7.27 £
non-repayable dividend rate	7.28 £	7.29 £	7.30 £
total foreign tax for which tax credit relief not claimed	7.31 £		

7.32 *Additional information*

Capital gains

The supplementary pages headed Capital gains cover all capital gains and losses whether from stocks and shares, land and buildings, or other assets in the UK and overseas.

You have to fill in these sheets if you sold or gave away assets of £15,400 or more and your chargeable gains for tax purposes were £7,700 or more in the year ended 5 April 2003.

To complete this section of the return you will need:

Copies of contract notes for the sale and purchase of shares	
Invoices and letters about the purchase and sale of other assets	
Invoices for all allowable expenses you can claim	

Chapter 16 of this book covers all aspects of capital gains.

Not all sections of the sheets are reproduced here. The first three pages of the capital gains sheets enable you to detail the relevant assets and then total them in boxes 8.1 to 8.6.

They are then summarised in boxes Q, U, L and O and 8.7 to 8.21 so as to record any gain or loss and any figures carried forward.

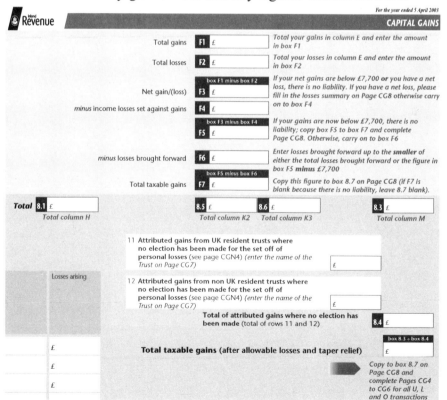

year | 8.2 £ [   ] ➤ Copy to box 8.10 on Page CG8 and, unless you need only complete the totals boxes (see page CGN5), complete column K1

Chargeable gains and allowable losses

Once you have completed Page CG1, or Pages CG2 to CG6, fill in this Page.

Have you 'ticked' any row in Column B, 'Tick box if estimate or valuation used' on Pages CG1 or CG2 or in Column C on Page CG2 'Tick box if asset held at 31 March 1982'? **YES**

Have you given details in Column G on Pages CG2 and CG3 of any Capital Gains reliefs claimed or due? **YES**

Are you claiming, and/or using, any clogged losses (see Notes, page CGN11)? **YES**

Enter from Page CG1 or column AA on Page CG2:

- the number of transactions in quoted shares or other securities box Q
- the number of transactions in other shares or securities box U
- the number of transactions in land and property box L
- the number of gains attributed to settlors box T
- the number of other transactions box O

Total taxable gains (from Page CG1 **or** Page CG3) 8.7 £

Your taxable gains *minus* the annual exempt amount of £7,700 (leave blank if '0' or negative) box 8.7 minus £7,700 8.8 £

Additional liability in respect of non-resident or dual resident trusts (see Notes, page CGN6) 8.9 £

Capital losses

(If your loss arose on a transaction with a connected person, see page CGN14, you can only set that loss against gains you make on disposals to that same connected person. See the notes on clogged losses on page CGN11.)

■ *This year's losses*

- Total (normally from box 8.2 on Page CG3 or box F2 on Page CG1. But, if you have clogged losses, see Notes, page CGN10) 8.10 £
- Used against gains (total of column K1 on Page CG3, or the smaller of boxes F1 and F2 on Page CG1) 8.11 £
- Used against earlier years' gains (generally only available to personal representatives, see Notes, page CGN11) 8.12 £
- Used against income (only losses of the type described on page CGN9 can be used against income) 8.13A £ amount claimed against income of 2002-03 / 8.13B £ amount claimed against income of 2001-02 box 8.13A + box 8.13B 8.13 £
- This year's unused losses box 8.10 minus (boxes 8.11 + 8.12 + 8.13) 8.14 £

■ *Summary of earlier years' losses*

- Unused losses of 1996-97 and later years 8.15 £
- Used this year (losses from box 8.15 are used in priority to losses from box 8.18) (column K3 on Page CG3 or box F6 on Page CG1) 8.16 £
- Remaining unused losses of 1996-97 and later years box 8.15 minus box 8.16 8.17 £
- Unused losses of 1995-96 and earlier years 8.18 £
- Used this year (losses from box 8.15 are used in priority to losses from box 8.18) (column K3 on Page CG3 or box F6 on Page CG1) box 8.6 minus box 8.16 (or box F6 minus box 8.16) 8.19 £

■ *Total of unused losses to carry forward*

- Carried forward losses of 1996-97 and later years box 8.14 + box 8.17 8.20 £
- Carried forward losses of 1995-96 and earlier years box 8.18 minus box 8.19 8.21 £

Non-residence etc.

The supplementary pages Non-residence etc. contain a sequence of questions to enable the tax office to determine whether you are:

- Not resident in the UK.
- Not ordinarily resident in the UK.
- Entitled to apportion income in the tax year.
- Not domiciled in the UK.

The rules governing the legal status of a person and the consequent tax implications are among some of the most difficult tax legislation and are outside the scope of this basic tax guide.

However, if you have requested these supplementary pages, the tax office will automatically send you a set of extensive notes to help you decide your tax status.

Note that not all sections of the forms are reproduced here.

Inland Revenue

For the year ended 5 April 2003

NON-RESIDENCE ETC.

Residence status

I am (please tick appropriate box)

- resident in the UK | 9.1
- ordinarily resident in the UK | 9.3
- not domiciled in the UK (and it is relevant to my Income Tax or Capital Gains Tax liability) | 9.5
- claiming personal allowances as a non-resident | 9.7

- not resident in the UK | 9.2
- not ordinarily resident in the UK | 9.4
- claiming split-year treatment | 9.6
- resident in a country other than the UK (under a double taxation agreement) at the same time as being resident in the UK | 9.8

Information required if you claim to be non-resident in the UK for the whole of 2002-03

- Are you in any of the following categories:

  - a Commonwealth citizen (this includes a British citizen) or an EEA (European Economic Area) national?
  - a present or former employee of the British Crown (including a civil servant, member of the armed forces etc)?
  - a UK missionary society employee?
  - a civil servant in a territory under the protection of the British Crown?
  - a resident of the Isle of Man or the Channel Islands?
  - a former resident of the UK and you live abroad for the sake of your own health or the health of a member of your family who lives with you?
  - a widow or widower of an employee of the British Crown?

    Yes | 9.9   No | 9.10

- How many days have you spent in the UK, excluding days of arrival and departure, during the year ended 5 April 2003? Enter the number of days | 9.11 | days

- Were you resident in the UK for 2001-02?   Yes | 9.12   No | 9.13

- How many days have you spent in the UK up to 5 April 2003, excluding days of arrival and departure, since 5 April 1999 or, if later, the date you originally left the UK ? Enter the number of days | 9.14 | days

- What is your country of nationality? | 9.15

- In which country are you resident? | 9.16

Information required if you claim to be not ordinarily resident in the UK for the whole of 2002-03

- Were you ordinarily resident in the UK for 2001-02?　　Yes 9.17　　No 9.18

- When you came to the UK, did you intend to stay here for at least three years?　　Yes 9.19　　No 9.20　　Not applicable 9.21

- If you have left the UK, do you intend to live outside the UK permanently?　　Yes 9.22　　No 9.23　　Not applicable 9.24

Information required if you claim split-year treatment

- Date of your arrival in the UK　　9.25　Day / Month / Year

- Date of your departure from the UK　　9.26　Day / Month / Year

Information required if you claim to be not domiciled in the UK

- Have you submitted full facts to the Inland Revenue (for example, on forms DOM1 or P86) regarding your domicile in the six years ended 5 April 2003?　　Yes 9.27　　No 9.28

- If you came to the UK before 6 April 2002, has there been a relevant change in your circumstances or intentions during the year ended 5 April 2003?　　Yes 9.29　　No 9.30　　Not appropriate 9.31

Information required if you are resident in the UK and you also claim to be resident in another country for the purposes of a Double Taxation Agreement

- In which country as well as the UK were you regarded as resident for 2002-03?　　9.32

- Were you also regarded as resident in the country in box 9.32 for 2001-02?　　Yes 9.33　　No 9.34

Information required if you are not resident or are resident in another country for the purpose of a Double Taxation Agreement and are claiming relief under a Double Taxation Agreement

- Amount of any relief you are claiming from UK tax if you are not resident in the UK or are dual resident　　9.35 £

You must fill in and send me the claim form in *Help Sheet IR302: Dual residents* or *Help Sheet IR304: Non residents - relief under Double Taxation Agreements* as applicable. These are available from the Orderline.

9.36 *Additional information*

Having completed any supplementary pages that are relevant, you can now fill in pages 3 and 4 of the *main tax return*. This section covers income from investments, pensions, social security benefits and any other income not covered under other sections of the return.

Savings income

The first section (Q10) covers income from savings and investments. To answer these questions you will need:

Interest statements and tax deduction certificates from UK banks, building societies and deposit takers	
Details of any National Savings investments	
Dividend vouchers showing tax credits	

Although the tax office does not want you to list all your individual dividends and interest etc. in the tax form – you only have to put in the totals – you will need to keep the details in case you are asked for them. See also page 62 for further advice.

INCOME *for the year ended 5 April 2003*

Q10 Did you receive any income from UK savings and investments? **YES** [ ]

If yes, tick this box and then fill in boxes 10.1 to 10.26 as appropriate. Include only your share from any joint savings and investments. If not applicable, go to Question 11.

■ *Interest*

● Interest from UK banks, building societies and deposit takers (interest from UK Internet accounts must be included) - *if you have more than one bank or building society etc account enter* **totals** *in the boxes.*

- enter any bank, building society etc interest that **has not** had tax taken off. (Most interest is taxed by your bank or building society etc. so make sure you should be filling in box 10.1, rather than boxes 10.2 to 10.4)

Taxable amount
10.1 £

- enter details of your **taxed** bank or building society etc interest. *The Working Sheet on page 10 of your Tax Return Guide will help you fill in boxes 10.2 to 10.4.*

Amount after tax deducted	Tax deducted	Gross amount before tax
10.2 £	**10.3** £	**10.4** £

● Interest distributions from UK authorised unit trusts and open-ended investment companies (dividend distributions go below)

Amount after tax deducted	Tax deducted	Gross amount before tax
10.5 £	**10.6** £	**10.7** £

● National Savings & Investments (other than First Option Bonds and Fixed Rate Savings Bonds and the first £70 of interest from an Ordinary Account)

Taxable amount
10.8 £

● National Savings & Investments First Option Bonds and Fixed Rate Savings Bonds

Amount after tax deducted	Tax deducted	Gross amount before tax
10.9 £	**10.10** £	**10.11** £

● Other income from UK savings and investments (except dividends)

Amount after tax deducted	Tax deducted	Gross amount before tax
10.12 £	**10.13** £	**10.14** £

■ *Dividends*

● Dividends and other qualifying distributions from UK companies

Dividend/distribution	Tax credit	Dividend/distribution plus credit
10.15 £	**10.16** £	**10.17** £

● Dividend distributions from UK authorised unit trusts and open-ended investment companies

Dividend/distribution	Tax credit	Dividend/distribution plus credit
10.18 £	**10.19** £	**10.20** £

● Scrip dividends from UK companies

Dividend	Notional tax	Dividend plus notional tax
10.21 £	**10.22** £	**10.23** £

● Non-qualifying distributions and loans written off

Distribution/Loan	Notional tax	Taxable amount
10.24 £	**10.25** £	**10.26** £

Pensions and benefits income

The next section (Q11) deals with UK pensions and social security benefits received. To fill in this section you will need:

Your State pension book or details	
A P60 form or certificate of tax deducted in the case of any other pension	
Benefit office statements in respect of unemployment benefit, income support or jobseeker's allowance	
Details of any incapacity benefit or other taxable State benefit	

Do not include the State Christmas bonus or winter fuel payment as they are not taxable. See page 90 for further details.

Q11 Did you receive a taxable UK pension, retirement annuity or Social Security benefit? YES
Read the notes on pages 13 to 15 of the Tax Return Guide.

■ *State pensions and benefits*

Taxable amount for 2002-03

- State Retirement Pension - *enter the total of your entitlements for the year* — **11.1** £
- Widow's Pension or Bereavement Allowance — **11.2** £
- Widowed Mother's Allowance or Widowed Parent's Allowance — **11.3** £
- Industrial Death Benefit Pension — **11.4** £
- Jobseeker's Allowance — **11.5** £
- Invalid Care Allowance — **11.6** £
- Statutory Sick Pay, Statutory Maternity Pay and Statutory Paternity Pay paid by the Inland Revenue — **11.7** £

	Tax deducted	Gross amount **before** tax
• Taxable Incapacity Benefit	**11.8** £	**11.9** £

■ *Other pensions and retirement annuities*

	Amount after tax deducted	Tax deducted	Gross amount **before** tax
• Pensions (other than State pensions) and retirement annuities - *if you have more than one pension or annuity, please add together and complete boxes 11.10 to 11.12. Provide details of each one in box 11.14*	**11.10** £	**11.11** £	**11.12** £

11.14

- Deduction - *see the note for box 11.13 on page 15 of your Tax Return Guide* — Amount of deduction **11.13** £

Other income

Sections Q12 and Q13 deal with any other income that you may have received. Refer to the index at the back of this book for help.

Q13 in particular is useful for declaring any miscellaneous income from casual work, insurance or mail order commission, royalties, consultancy work etc., but make sure you claim any allowable expenses (see page 57) and only put the net figure in your tax return.

You must have kept details of all your expenses for, although the Inland Revenue don't need you to give a breakdown in the tax return, they may ask you questions at a later date.

There is an additional information box (23.5) later in your tax return if there is insufficient room in this section.

Q12 Did you make any gains on UK life insurance policies, life annuities or capital redemption policies or receive refunds of surplus funds from additional voluntary contributions? | **YES** [ ] | If yes, tick this box and then fill in boxes 12.1 to 12.12 as appropriate. If not applicable, go to Question 13.

- Gains on UK annuities and friendly societies' life insurance policies where no tax is treated as paid

  Number of years **12.1** [ ]   Amount of gain(s) **12.2** £ [ ]

- Gains on UK life insurance policies etc. on which tax is treated as paid - *read pages 15 to 18 of your Tax Return Guide*

  Number of years **12.3** [ ]   Tax treated as paid **12.4** £ [ ]   Amount of gain(s) **12.5** £ [ ]

- Gains on life insurance policies in ISAs that have been made void

  12.6 [ ]   Tax deducted **12.7** £ [ ]   Amount of gain(s) **12.8** £ [ ]

- Corresponding deficiency relief

  Amount **12.9** £ [ ]

- Refunds of surplus funds from additional voluntary contributions

  Amount received **12.10** £ [ ]   Notional tax **12.11** £ [ ]   Amount plus notional tax **12.12** £ [ ]

Q13 Did you receive any other taxable income which you have not already entered elsewhere in your Tax Return? | **YES** [ ] | If yes, tick this box and then fill in boxes 13.1 to 13.6 as appropriate. If not applicable, go to Question 14.

Fill in any supplementary Pages before answering Question 13.
(Supplementary Pages follow page 10, or are available from the Orderline.)

- Other taxable income – also provide details in box 23.5 - *read the notes on pages 18 to 20 of your Tax Return Guide*

  Amount after tax deducted **13.1** £ [ ]   Tax deducted **13.2** £ [ ]   Amount before tax **13.3** £ [ ]

- Tick box 13.1A if box 13.1 includes enhanced capital allowances for environmentally friendly expenditure

  13.1A [ ]   Losses brought forward **13.4** £ [ ]   Earlier years' losses used in 2002-03 **13.5** £ [ ]

  2002-03 losses carried forward **13.6** £ [ ]

Reliefs

Having dealt with the income from all sources, the tax return now covers reliefs and allowances that you can claim as a deduction from your income.

First, the reliefs. Q14 covers relief for pension contributions. Refer to page 128 for clarification on the various types of pension scheme currently available.

To fill in Q14 you will need:

Pension statements from the insurance company or from the trustees of your employer's scheme	

RELIEFS *for the year ended 5 April 2003*

Q14 Do you want to claim relief for your pension contributions? | **YES** [ ] | If yes, tick this box and then fill in boxes 14.1 to 14.11 as appropriate. If not appliable, go to Question 15

Do not include contributions deducted from your pay by your employer to their pension scheme or associated AVC scheme, because tax relief is given automatically. But do include your contributions to personal pension schemes and Free-Standing AVC schemes.

■ **Payments to your retirement annuity contracts - only fill in boxes 14.1 to 14.5 for policies taken out before 1 July 1988.**
  See the notes on page 20 of your Tax Return Guide.

Qualifying payments made in 2002-03 **14.1** £ [ ]	2002-03 payments used in an earlier year **14.2** £ [ ]	Relief claimed
2002-03 payments now to be carried back **14.3** £ [ ]	Payments brought back from 2003-04 **14.4** £ [ ]	box 14.1 *minus* (boxes 14.2 and 14.3, but not 14.4) **14.5** £ [ ]

■ **Payments to your personal pension (including stakeholder pension) contracts** - *enter the amount of the payment you made with the basic rate tax added (the **gross** payment). See the note for box 14.6 on page 22 of your Tax Return Guide.*

Gross qualifying payments made in 2002-03	**14.6** £	
2002-03 gross payments carried back to 2001-02	**14.7** £	Relief claimed
		box 14.6 *minus* box 14.7 (but not 14.8)
Gross qualifying payments made between 6 April 2003 and 31 January 2004 brought back to 2002-03 - *see page 22 of your Tax Return Guide*	**14.8** £	**14.9** £

■ **Contributions to other pension schemes and Free-Standing AVC schemes**

• Amount of contributions to employer's schemes **not deducted** at source from pay	**14.10** £
• Gross amount of Free-Standing Additional Voluntary Contributions paid in 2002-03	**14.11** £

Boxes **14.1** to **14.11** see pages 128 to 130.

The next question, Q15, covers all other reliefs. To fill this in you will need:

Statements or certificates from third parties

Q15 **Do you want to claim any of the following reliefs?**
If you have made any annual payments, after basic rate tax, answer 'Yes' to Question 15 and fill in box 15.9. If you have made any gifts to charity go to Question 15A

YES

If yes, tick this box and then fill in boxes 15.1 to 15.12, as appropriate.
If not applicable, go to Question 15A

• Interest eligible for relief on qualifying loans	**15.1** £
• Maintenance or alimony payments you have made under a court order, Child Support Agency assessment or legally binding order or agreement	Amount claimed up to £2,110 **15.2** £
To claim this relief, either you or your former spouse must have been 65 or over on 5 April 2000. So, if **your** date of birth, which is entered in box 22.6, is after 5 April 1935 then you must enter your former **spouse's** date of birth in box 15.2A - *see page 23 of your Tax Return Guide*	Former spouse's date of birth **15.2A** / /
• Subscriptions for Venture Capital Trust shares (up to £100,000)	Amount on which relief is claimed **15.3** £
• Subscriptions under the Enterprise Investment Scheme (up to £150,000) - *also provide details in box 23.5, see page 24 of your Tax Return Guide*	Amount on which relief is claimed **15.4** £
• Community Investment Tax relief - invested amount relating to previous tax year(s) and on which relief is due	**15.5** £	Total amount on which relief is claimed box 15.5 + box 15.6
• Community Investment Tax relief - invested amount for current tax year	**15.6** £	**15.7** £
• Post-cessation expenses, pre-incorporation losses brought forward and losses on relevant discounted securities, etc. - *see page 24 of your Tax Return Guide*	Amount of payment **15.8** £
• Annuities and annual payments	Payments made **15.9** £
• Payments to a trade union or friendly society for death benefits	Half amount of payment **15.10** £
• Payment to your employer's compulsory widow's, widower's or orphan's benefit scheme - *available in some circumstances – **first** read the notes on page 25 of your Tax Return Guide*	Relief claimed **15.11** £
• Relief claimed on a qualifying distribution on the **redemption** of bonus shares or securities.	Relief claimed **15.12** £

Box no. **15.1** see page 64.   Box no. **15.5** see page 127.

Box no. **15.2** see page 65.   Box no. **15.6** see page 127.

Box no. **15.3** see page 127.   Box no. **15.7** see page 127.

Box no. **15.4** see page 126.   Box no. **15.8** see page 105.

Box no. **15.9** see page 64. Box no. **15.11** see page 67.

Box no. **15.10** see page 67. Box no. **15.12** see page 11.

Allowances

The allowances section of the return (Q15A and Q16) is your chance to claim relief on gifts to charity, the married couple's allowance, the blind person's allowance or the children's tax credit.

Refer to page 66 for the various methods you can use to give to charity in a tax-efficient way.

Chapter 9 gives background details to all these allowances including the option you have to transfer surplus allowances to your wife or husband. Boxes 16.14 to 16.33 cover the children's tax credit (see page 70).

ALLOWANCES for the year ended 5 April 2003

Q15A **Do you want to claim relief on gifts to charity?** | **YES** | If yes, tick this box and then read page 26 of your Tax Return Guide. Fill in boxes 15A.1 to 15A.5 as appropriate. If not applicable, go to Question 16.
If you have made any Gift Aid payments answer 'Yes' to Question 15A. You should include Gift Aid payments to Community Amateur Sports Clubs here. You can elect to include in this Return Gift Aid payments made between 6 April 2003 and the date you send in this Return. See page 26 in the Tax Return Guide and the leaflet enclosed.

- Gift Aid and payments under charitable covenants made between 6 April 2002 and 5 April 2003 — **15A.1** £
- Enter in box 15A.2 the total of any 'one off' payments included in box 15A.1 — **15A.2** £
- Enter in box 15A.3 the amount of Gift Aid payments made after 5 April 2003 but treated as if made in the tax year 2002-03 — **15A.3** £
- Gifts of qualifying investments to charities – shares and securities — **15A.4** £
- Gifts of qualifying investments to charities – real property — **15A.5** £

Q16 **Do you want to claim blind person's allowance, married couple's allowance or the Children's Tax Credit?** | **YES** | If yes, tick this box and then read pages 26 to 31 of your Tax Return Guide. Fill in boxes 16.1 to 16.33 as appropriate. If not applicable, go to Question 17.
You get your personal allowance of £4,615 automatically. **If you were born before 6 April 1938, enter your date of birth in box 22.6** - you may get a higher age-related personal allowance.

	Date of registration (if first year of claim)		Local authority (or other register)
■ *Blind person's allowance*	**16.1** / /		**16.2**

■ *Married couple's allowance* - In 2002-03 married couple's allowance can only be claimed if either you, or your husband or wife, were born **before 6 April 1935**. So you can only claim the allowance in 2002-03 if either of you had reached **65 years of age before 6 April 2000**. Further guidance is given beginning on page 27 of your Tax Return Guide.

If **both** you and your husband or wife were born after 5 April 1935 you cannot claim; **do not** complete boxes 16.3 to 16.13.

If **you can claim** fill in boxes 16.3 and 16.4 if you are a married man or if you are a married woman and you are claiming half or all of the married couple's allowance.

- Enter your date of birth (if born before 6 April 1935) — **16.3** / /
- Enter your spouse's date of birth (**if** born before 6 April 1935 **and** if older than you) — **16.4** / /

Then, if you are a married man fill in boxes 16.5 to 16.9. If you are a married woman fill in boxes 16.10 to 16.13.

- Wife's full name — **16.5** — ● Date of marriage (if after 5 April 2002) — **16.6** / /

	Half	All
● Tick box 16.7, or box 16.8, if you or your wife have allocated half, or all, of the minimum amount of the allowance to her	**16.7**	**16.8**

- Enter in box 16.9 the date of birth of any previous wife with whom you lived at any time during 2002-03. Read 'Special rules if you are a man who married in the year ended 5 April 2003' on page 27 before completing box 16.9. — **16.9** / /

	Half	All
● Tick box 16.10, or box 16.11, if you or your husband have allocated half, or all, of the minimum amount of the allowance to you	**16.10**	**16.11**

- Husband's full name — **16.12** — ● Date of marriage (if after 5 April 2002) — **16.13** / /

ALLOWANCES *for the year ended 5 April 2003, continued*

■ **Children's Tax Credit** – *even if you have already completed a separate Children's Tax Credit (CTC) claim form and received the relief in your tax code, you should still fill in boxes 16.14 to 16.26, as directed. Any reference to 'partner' in this question means the person you lived with during the year to 5 April 2003 – your husband or wife, or someone you lived with as husband or wife.*

Guidance for claiming CTC is on pages 28 to 31 of your Tax Return Guide. Please read the notes before completing your claim, particularly if either you, or your partner, were liable to tax above the basic rate in the year to 5 April 2003.

● Enter in box 16.14 the date of birth of a child living with you who was born on or after 6 April 1986.
If you have a child living with you who was born on or after 6 April 2002 make sure you enter their date of birth in this box in preference to claiming for an older child.

| 16.14 | / | / |

● Tick box 16.15 if the child was your own child or one you looked after at your own expense.
If not, you cannot claim CTC – go to box 16.27, if appropriate, or Question 17.

16.15

● Tick box 16.16 if the child lived with you **throughout** the year to 5 April 2003.
If you ticked box 16.16 and
- you were a lone or single claimant, you have finished this question; go to Question 17,
- you have a partner, go to box 16.18.

16.16

● If the child lived with you for only **part of the year** you may only be entitled to a proportion of the CTC.
Enter in box 16.17 your share in £s that **you have agreed** with any other claimants that you may claim for this child. But leave boxes 16.17 to 16.25 blank if you separated from, or started living with, your partner during the year to 5 April 2003. Special rules apply to work out your entitlement; ask the Orderline for *Help Sheet IR343: Claiming Children's Tax Credit when your circumstances change* which explains how to complete box 16.26.

16.17 £

● I had the higher income and I am claiming all of our entitlement to CTC

16.23

● We are both making separate claims for half of our entitlement to CTC

16.24

● We elected before 6 April 2002, or because of our special circumstances, during the year to 5 April 2003 (see page 31 of your Tax Return Guide), for the partner with the lower income to claim all of our entitlement to CTC

16.25

● If you separated from, or starting living with, your partner in the year to 5 April 2003, enter in box 16.26 the amount of CTC you are claiming *(following the guidance in Help Sheet IR343: Claiming Children's Tax Credit when your circumstances change.)*

16.26 £

■ *Transfer of surplus allowances - see page 31 of your Tax Return Guide before you fill in boxes 16.27 to 16.33.*

● Tick box 16.27 if you want your spouse to have your unused allowances

16.27

● Tick box 16.28 if you want to have your spouse's unused allowances

16.28

● Tick box 16.29 if you want to have your partner's unused CTC

16.29

● Tick box 16.30 if your surplus CTC should be transferred to your partner

16.30

Please give details in the 'Additional information' box, box 23.5, on page 9 - *see page 31 of your Tax Return Guide for what is needed.*

If you want to calculate your tax, enter the amount of the surplus allowance you can have.

● Blind person's surplus allowance

16.31 £

● Married couple's surplus allowance

16.32 £

● Surplus CTC

16.33 £

OTHER INFORMATION *for the year ended 5 April 2003*

Q17 **Are you liable to make Student Loan Repayments for 2002-03 on an Income Contingent Student Loan?**
You must read the note on page 31 of your Tax Return Guide before ticking the 'Yes' box.

YES

If yes, and you are calculating your tax enter in Question 18, box 18.2A the amount you work out is repayable in 2002-03

Refer to page 74 for student loan information.

Other information

The final section of your tax return, headed other information, asks some general questions (Q18–Q22).

You must decide here whether you want to calculate your own tax liability (or refund).

If you do, you can either use the tax calculation sheets sent with your tax return, which are very comprehensive as they have to cover all conceivable situations, or you can use the *Check Your Tax* calculator on pages 133–136 of this book.

OTHER INFORMATION *for the year ended 5 April 2003, continued*

Q18 Do you want to calculate your tax and, if appropriate, any Student Loan Repayment? **YES** ☐ Use your Tax Calculation Guide then fill in boxes 18.1 to 18.8 as appropriate.

- Unpaid tax for earlier years **included in your tax code for 2002-03** **18.1** £
- Tax due for 2002-03 included in your tax code for a later year **18.2** £
- Student Loan Repayment due **18.2A** £
- Total tax, Class 4 NIC and Student Loan Repayment due for 2002-03 **before** you made any payments on account *(put the amount in brackets if an overpayment)* **18.3** £
- Tax due for earlier years **18.4** £
- Tax overpaid for earlier years **18.5** £
- Tick box 18.6 if you are claiming to reduce your 2003-04 payments on account. Make sure you enter the **reduced** amount of your first payment in box 18.7. Then, in the 'Additional information' box, box 23.5 on page 9, say why you are making a claim **18.6** ☐
- Your first payment on account for 2003-04 *(include the pence)* **18.7** £
- Any 2003-04 tax you are reclaiming now **18.8** £

Under section Q19, if you think a repayment of tax is due to you, then fill in the relevant personal information.

Q20 to Q22 also need completing, showing any tax refunded or set off, and your personal details.

Q19 Do you want to claim a repayment if you have paid too **much tax?** *(If you do not tick 'Yes' or the tax you have overpaid is below £10, I will use the amount you are owed to reduce your next tax bill.)* **YES** ☐ **If yes,** tick this box and then fill in boxes 19.1 to 19.12 as appropriate. If not applicable, go to Question 20.

Should the repayment be sent:

- to your bank or building society account?
  Tick box 19.1 and fill in boxes 19.3 to 19.7 **19.1**
or
- to your nominee's bank or building society account? *Tick box 19.2 and fill in boxes 19.3 to 19.12* **19.2**

We prefer to make repayment direct into a bank or building society account. (But tick box 19.8A or box 19.8B if you would like a cheque to be sent to you or your nominee.)

Name of bank or building society
19.3

Branch sort code
19.4

Account number
19.5

Name of account holder
19.6

Building society reference
19.7

If you would like a cheque to be sent to:

- you, at the address on page 1, tick box 19.8A **19.8A**
or
- your nominee, tick box 19.8B **19.8B**

If your nominee is your agent, tick box 19.9A **19.9A**

Agent's reference for you (if your nominee is your agent)
19.9

I authorise

Name of your nominee/agent
19.10

Nominee/agent address
19.11

Postcode

to receive on my behalf the amount due

19.12 *This authority must be signed by you. A photocopy of your signature will not do.*

Signature

OTHER INFORMATION *for the year ended 5 April 2003, continued*

Q20 Have you already had any 2002-03 tax refunded or set off
by your Inland Revenue office or the Benefits Agency
(in Northern Ireland, the Social Security Agency)?
Read the notes on page 32 of your Tax Return Guide

YES ☐

20.1 £ _____

Q21 Is your name or address on the front of the Tax Return *wrong*?
*If you are filling in an approved substitute Tax Return, see the notes on
page 32 of the Tax Return Guide*

YES ☐

Q22 Please give other personal details in boxes 22.1 to 22.7. *This information helps us to be more efficient and effective.*

Your daytime telephone number	Your first two forenames
22.1	22.4

Your agent's telephone number	Say if you are single, married, widowed, divorced or separated
22.2	22.5

and their name and address

22.3

Your date of birth (If you were born before 6 April 1938, you may
get a higher age-related allowance.)

22.6 / /

Your National Insurance number
(if known and not on page 1 of your Tax Return)

22.7

Postcode

The final page of the tax return asks some general questions so that the tax office knows how to handle your tax affairs or how to calculate your tax code for 2003–2004.

Q23 asks for additional information generally, and box 23.1 in particular, gives you the option of *not* paying any tax liability due through your PAYE tax code – for example you may not want your employer to know that you have other income or have made other profits or gains.

Q23 Please tick boxes 23.1 to 23.4 if they apply. Provide any additional information in box 23.5 below
(continue on page 10, if necessary).

Tick box 23.1 if you do **not** want any tax you owe for 2002-03 collected through your tax code. **23.1** ☐

Please tick box 23.2 if this Tax Return contains figures that are provisional because you do not yet have final figures.
Pages 32 and 33 of the Tax Return Guide explain the circumstances in which provisional figures may be used and asks for
some additional information to be provided in box 23.5 below. **23.2** ☐

Tick box 23.3 if you are claiming relief now for 2003-04 trading, or certain capital, losses. Enter in box 23.5 the
amount and year. **23.3** ☐

Tick box 23.4 if you are claiming to have post-cessation or other business receipts taxed as income of an earlier
year. Enter in box 23.5 the amount and year. **23.4** ☐

23.5 *Additional information*

Finally, tick the boxes under Q24 to indicate any supplementary pages you are attaching to your tax return. For employment, self-employment and partnership supplementary pages you will also need to indicate the number of sets of pages included. Then sign and date the declaration.

OTHER INFORMATION *for the year ended 5 April 2003, continued*

Q24 Declaration

I have filled in and am sending back to you the following pages:

Tick

In the second box enter the number of **complete sets** *of supplementary Pages enclosed*

1 TO 10 OF THIS FORM	Number of sets				
EMPLOYMENT		PARTNERSHIP		TRUSTS, ETC	
SHARE SCHEMES	Number of sets	LAND & PROPERTY		CAPITAL GAINS	
SELF-EMPLOYMENT		FOREIGN		NON-RESIDENCE, ETC	

Tick Number of sets

Tick

Before you send your completed Tax Return back to your Inland Revenue office, you must sign the statement below. If you give false information or conceal any part of your income or chargeable gains, you may be liable to financial penalties and/or you may be prosecuted.

24.1 The information I have given in this Tax Return is correct and complete to the best of my knowledge and belief.

Signature   Date

When you sign your tax return you are declaring that to the best of your knowledge, the return is complete, true and accurate.

It is often thought that if you keep quiet about some of your income, then the tax inspector will not find out about it. This is not the case. The tax authorities have many sources of information, the most common being your employer, banks, building societies and other businesses, all of whom may be required to make a return of payments made to individuals and businesses.

What if you have made a mistake?

Do not worry if you have forgotten to claim an allowance due to you, for you have a time limit of five years from the relevant 31 January date in which to tell your tax office of your mistake and claim a refund.

If you forget to include some of your income on the form, you should immediately notify your tax office explaining your error.

When to send in your tax return

If you want the tax office to calculate your tax liability or refund for 2002–2003, you must send in your tax return by 30 September 2003 (or it is likely this will be extended to 30 December 2003 if filed electronically via the internet). They will then send you a statement by 31 January 2004.

If you wish to use the tax calculator and calculate your own tax liability (see page 132), then you have until 31 January 2004 to send in your return; you should also pay the tax that you think is due.

You can send in your tax return electronically on the internet (www.inlandrevenue.gov.uk) if you wish and if you use the website the calculations are done interactively. Remember that you must remain on line for the entire time you are filling in the form, so make sure you have all the information to hand; also as the filing deadline approaches, the website is likely to be busy and access may be slow.

Payments on account

If you have several sources of untaxed income or you are self-employed, you will have to make two payments on account for each tax year. For example, for the year ended 5 April 2003 the first payment of 50 per cent of your anticipated tax bill should have been made by 31 January 2003 and the second 50 per cent on 31 July 2003; any balance due, once your tax liability is agreed, being payable on 31 January 2004, although a refund may be dealt with as soon as agreed.

It is up to you to work out how much you need to pay on account. If you disagree with any figure that the tax office has demanded, then ask for form SA 303 on which you can explain your reasons.

Surcharges and penalties

There will be an automatic penalty of £100 if your tax return is not sent in by 31 January 2004 and another £100 six months later if it is still overdue. These are reduced if the tax due is less than £200. However, a tribunal may award a penalty of up to £60 a day and, if the return is 12 months late, there is a further penalty of up to 100 per cent of the tax liability.

In addition, a surcharge may arise on any tax paid late – 5 per cent of any tax due by 31 January if unpaid at 28 February, and a further 5 per cent if unpaid by 31 July (plus interest on the first surcharge).

There are also fines of up to £3,000 for each failure to keep adequate records to support figures in your tax return.

Problems with your tax office

Contact your tax enquiry office initially if you have a query; then your tax inspector. If you still do not get satisfaction, write to the District Inspector or Regional Controller or as a last resort the Inland Revenue adjudicator.

Keep your records

The law requires you to keep all records of earnings, income, benefits, profits and expenses, etc. and all relevant information for 22 months from the end of the tax year and five years and ten months if you are self-employed.

CHAPTER 5

Your 2003 tax return
Pay, perks and pensions

This chapter deals with income from employment including any benefits or expense allowances, and redundancy or leaving compensation you have received. Any pensions and social security benefits are also covered here.

Wages, salaries, fees, bonuses, etc.

You should have received from your employer a form P60 which shows your earnings for the year and tax deducted under PAYE. You are entitled by law to receive this form by 31 May so chase your employer if it is not to hand.

Also include in the Employment section of the tax return any wages you received from your husband or wife if you were employed in his or her business.

You must show your gross earnings before any deductions of income tax and national insurance, but you are allowed to deduct any contributions you make to your employer's pension scheme provided that it is one approved by the tax inspector.

Your P60 form may include pay from a previous employer, in which case it needs to be shown on a separate Employment page as you need one for each employer; or it may include payments for unemployment benefits, income support or jobseeker's allowance: these must be shown separately on page four, the Income section of your tax return.

Directors' remuneration is frequently voted on an annual basis. The amount to show in your tax return is usually the amount actually received in the tax year (normally the figure on your P60 form); however, you are taxable on earnings shown in the company's accounts if such sums were *available* (even if not actually drawn by you) in the tax year.

In addition to your regular PAYE employment, you may have other earnings. These might include casual work, fees and commissions, etc. Do not enter such income in this section, but under the Income section of your tax return (Q13) – see page 39 in this book. Make sure you claim any relevant expenses (see page 57).

Tips and gratuities, if not included in your P60 form, should, however, be shown in box 1.9.

If you are employed, then you must keep all records of earnings, income, benefits and expenses, etc. for 22 months after the end of the tax year.

Benefits

Company cars

Virtually all employees whose earnings, and reimbursed expenses *including* potential benefits in kind, are at the rate of £8,500 a year or more, and all directors whatever their earnings and expenses, are liable to pay tax on the 'benefit' they have from the use of a company car, and additionally on any fuel used on private journeys if paid for by their employer. These benefits will still be taxable if the car is used by a member of the employee's family or household. Company car and fuel benefits should appear in your coding notice or tax assessment and need to be checked against the information provided by your employer.

The car benefit tax applies to all company cars, including those that are leased, and they will be assumed by your tax office to cover all the running costs, even if these amount to more than the tax benefit charge. The cost of a chauffeur, however, will be taxed as a separate benefit.

A taxable benefit will not usually arise if a company car is part of a 'pool', provided that the vehicle is actually used by two or more employees, with any private use being merely incidental, and the vehicle is not normally kept overnight at or near the employee's place of residence.

If a company car is not available for a period of at least 30 consecutive days (for example, if it is in for repair), then the car benefit is reduced proportionately.

Company car benefit for 2002–2003 onwards

A new system for taxing car benefits started on 6 April 2002. (See Appendix 1, page 136, for the benefit calculations prior to this.)

The tax charge on the benefit is calculated as a percentage of the list price of the car, but this percentage is graduated according to carbon dioxide (CO_2) emissions.

There is no reduction for business mileage, and the age of the car is irrelevant.

The value of the vehicle for tax purposes is the manufacturer's list price at the time of first registration (less any personal contribution up to £5,000) and including delivery charges, VAT and any accessories over £100 added to the vehicle, unless they were for disabled persons. There are exceptions for classic cars; the open market value is taken instead of the list price where the car is aged 15 years or more at the end of the tax year and has a market value of £15,000 or more. (There is a cap of £80,000 on the list, or market, price.)

The minimum normal charge will be 15 per cent of the list price for cars with the lowest CO_2 emissions with a maximum of 35 per cent for cars with high emissions. Cars without an approved emissions figure (i.e. all cars registered before 1 January 1998) will be taxed according to engine size (see table below). Discounts are available for cars that run on alternative fuels and technologies. Ask the Inland Revenue for leaflet IR172 if you require more information.

Your car's emission figure will either be in the vehicle registration document or available from the manufacturer or dealer, or enquire free of charge on the internet at www.smmt.co.uk, or if the car was registered after March 2001, www.vcacarfueldata.org.uk.

It is important to note that the starting point in the CO_2 table is reduced each year, so your benefit will normally increase each year.

Cars with approved CO_2 emissions rating

CO₂ emissions in grammes per kilometre			Taxable benefit
2002–2003	2003–2004	2004–2005	per cent
165	155	145	15*
170	160	150	16*
175	165	155	17*
180	170	160	18*
185	175	165	19*
190	180	170	20*
195	185	175	21*
200	190	180	22*
205	195	185	23*
210	200	190	24*
215	205	195	25*
220	210	200	26*
225	215	205	27*
230	220	210	28*
235	225	215	29*
240	230	220	30*
245	235	225	31*
250	240	230	32*
255	245	235	33**
260	250	240	34***
265	255	245	35****

Cars with no approved CO_2 emissions rating

Engine size (c.c.)	Pre-1998 car per cent	1998 or later car per cent
0–1,400	15	15*
1,401–2,000	22	25*
2,001 and over†	32	35****

Notes: Diesel supplements if car runs solely on diesel (waived if Euro 4 diesels):
* Add 3 per cent; **add 2 per cent; ***add 1 per cent; **** maximum charge so no diesel supplement.
† Also including rotary engined petrol cars which have no cylinder capacity.

Company car private fuel benefit

If your employer pays for fuel used on private journeys (and this includes travel from home to your normal business address), then you are taxed on the benefits regardless of your annual business mileage.

New regulations apply from 6 April 2003. A standard figure of £14,400 will be used and the tax benefit will be based on the CO_2 rating percentage of your vehicle (see table on page 49).

For example, if you have a vehicle with CO_2 emissions of 195 for 2003–2004, then the taxable benefit will be 23 per cent $\times$ £14,400 = £3,312. The private fuel benefit charges for previous years are shown in Appendix 1 on page 136.

Is there any way you can avoid the fuel tax charge? Yes – you can pay for *all* your own private fuel (or reimburse your employer for *all* the private usage) but if you do this you will have to keep a detailed record each year of every car journey undertaken, both private and business. Bear in mind that travel from your home to your normal place of business is considered to be private mileage for tax purposes.

You may well find it to your advantage to accept the tax charge – it might be less than you would actually pay for private mileage!

The tax charge is the maximum that can be levied, even if in practice the cost of private mileage is more.

Company vans

Employees benefiting from the private use of a company van pay income tax on a standard 'benefit' of £500 a year (£350 for vans four or more years old). There is no fuel charge.

The benefit is apportioned in the case of shared vans. The Inland Revenue are in the process of reviewing this charge and new rules are likely to be introduced from 6 April 2004.

Mileage allowances

Since 6 April 2002, a new system of statutory mileage rates has been in operation. The previous c.c. graduation was abolished and you can only claim 40p per mile for the first 10,000 business miles in a tax year, and 25p a mile thereafter; this is called 'approved mileage allowance payment' (AMAP); any payment over these figures will be subject to tax and NI.

If your employer reimburses less than the mileage figure above, then you can claim the difference in your tax return.

An extra 5p per mile can be paid by your employer if you have a business passenger, but you cannot claim relief for this if your employer doesn't pay it.

There is no longer an option to claim deductions based on *actual* expenditure and the Fixed Profit Car Scheme has also been abolished. You will only need to declare the mileage payments you receive if they are in excess of the Inland Revenue approved figures.

The motorcycle rates are 24p per business mile and 20p for bicycles for 2003–2004.

Mileage allowances for previous years are shown in Appendix 1.

Living accommodation

Unless there are exceptional circumstances, living accommodation provided by an employer is taxable as a benefit.

The amount assessed will normally equate to the gross rateable value of the property, but if the cost of the property is higher than £75,000 then an *additional* amount is taxable, based on the market value of the property, less £75,000, multiplied by the official rate of interest (this interest rate is laid down by the Inland Revenue).

Any rent or contribution to upkeep you made to your employer is deductible from the benefit before calculating tax due.

Low-interest loan

An employee who has the benefit of a cheap or interest-free loan is taxable on the benefit as compared with the official rate of interest. Since 6 April 2000, your employer has not needed to report loans if the whole of the interest would have been liable for tax relief.

If the total of non-eligible loans does not exceed £5,000 at any time in the tax year or if the loan is made on commercial terms and your employer supplies goods or services on credit to the general public, then no charge is made.

Other benefits

All employees whose earnings, expenses and potential benefits are at the rate of £8,500 a year or more, and most directors regardless of their earnings or expenses, will probably have had any benefits or perks they have received reported to the tax inspector by their employer. The employer has to do this by law by sending in a form P11D, of which you are entitled to receive a copy by 6 July. However, it is still your responsibility to declare such a perk in your tax return. There are certain benefits or perks which an employer can provide which are tax free. You need not mention them on your tax return if they are not taxable, but see page 59 for dispensations, etc.

Some of the more usual benefits, with a summary of the tax situation, are detailed overleaf.

Benefits

Benefit	Employees earning £8,500 a year or more and directors	Employees earning less than £8,500 a year
Assets provided for your use free of charge (e.g. video)	Taxable at 20 per cent of initial market value	Usually tax free
Canteen facilities available to directors and staff	Not taxable	
Car parking facilities at work	Not taxable	
Cash vouchers	Taxable	
Child care facilities (see page 73)	Not taxable	
Clothing and other goods given by your employer	Taxable	Taxed on secondhand value
Company cars, vans, etc.	Taxable	Not taxable
Computer equipment	Not taxable on first £2,500 of computer's value	
Credit cards (for personal, not business expenditure)	Taxable	
Exam prizes	Not taxable if reasonable and not part of employment contract	
Fuel for private use	Taxable at scale rate on company cars	Not taxable
Holidays	Taxable apart from business element	If employer pays directly, tax-free
Interest-free loan	Normally taxable	Not taxable
In-house benefits	Taxable only on the value of the marginal or additional cost to the employer	
Living accommodation	Normally taxable at annual value unless essential for your employment	
Luncheon vouchers	Tax free up to 15p per working day	
Mobile telephones	Not taxable if employer provides	
Outplacement counselling	Not taxable	
Pension contributions and death in service cover	Normally tax-free	
Private health schemes	Taxable	Not taxable
Prizes and incentive awards	Taxable	
Relocation expenses	Tax-free up to £8,000 (if qualifying)	
Scholarships provided by employers' trust	Taxable	Not taxable
Season tickets for travel paid directly by employer	Taxable	
Share incentive schemes	Not taxable	
Sick pay schemes	Taxable	
Travel to work by bus (free or discounted)	Not taxable	
Workplace sports facilities	Not taxable	

Leaving payments and compensation

Compensation for loss of office, payment in lieu of notice, ex-gratia payments, redundancy pay and retirement and death lump sums all come under this heading in the tax return.

The first £30,000 of compensation is tax free, but any excess is taxable. (This £30,000 limit has not been increased since 1988!)

Note, however, that if your contract of employment gives you a right to compensation on ceasing to be employed, then the lump sum you receive will be taxable, regardless of the amount.

When considering agreements for compensation, it is wise to consult a tax adviser or solicitor to negotiate the terms and the timing, which can be critical, especially on termination of a contract.

Any benefits arising after termination will be taxed only when they are actually received or 'enjoyed', rather than being taken into account in the actual redundancy year.

An example follows of the various tax calculations that have to be considered when assessing the impact of redundancy pay. In the example shown, when John sends in his 2003 self assessment tax return he will include the redundancy payment and will pay any tax due to the tax office by 31 January 2004.

An example of the tax calculations arising on the receipt of redundancy pay

John was made redundant during the 2002–2003 tax year. His total earnings for the year were £34,600 and he was awarded a redundancy payment of £90,000.

			£
Earnings			34,600
Less: Personal allowance, say			4,615
			29,985
Tax liability	£ 1,920 at 10 per cent		192
	£27,980 at 22 per cent		6,156
	£ 85 at 40 per cent		34
	£29,985	Tax due	6,382

A redundancy payment of £90,000 is to be made after the form P45 has been issued. The employer will deduct tax as follows:

	£
Redundancy	90,000
Less: Tax-free limit	30,000
	60,000
Less: Tax on £60,000 at 22 per cent	13,200
	£46,800

Once the employer has notified the tax office of this redundancy payment, they will then review the tax position as follows:

		£
Earnings		34,600
Add: Redundancy after tax-free limit		60,000
		94,600
Less: Personal allowance		4,615
		89,985
Tax liability calculated as:		£
£ 1,920 at 10 per cent		192
£27,980 at 22 per cent		6,156
£60,085 at 40 per cent		24,034
	£	30,382
Less: Tax already collected (as above)	6,382	
Deducted from redundancy payment	13,200	19,582
Additional tax due		£10,800

Expense allowances

Round-sum allowances are taxable as income unless an employee (and such term includes a director) can identify accurately the expenditure involved and satisfy the tax office that such sums were spent wholly, exclusively and necessarily on the employer's business.

Refer also to Chapter 6 – Claiming expenses against your income.

Share schemes

There are many share schemes that now offer tax incentives to encourage employees' involvement in companies, but the rules are complicated and will vary from scheme to scheme.

Savings-related share schemes (save as you earn)

Employees pay a monthly sum via their employer into a savings-related share option scheme over a predetermined period at the end of which, the savings, plus a tax-free bonus, are used to purchase shares at a fixed price. This price must not be less than 80 per cent of the market value at the time of the option. No income tax or National Insurance should be payable on the option grant or on exercising the option.

No capital gain arises if shares up to the value of £3,000 are transferred into an ISA within certain time limits, and this applied similarly to PEPs (up to the annual limit) prior to 6 April 1999.

All-employee share ownership plans

These new plans took effect from April 2000 whereby companies could set up an all-employee share ownership plan, with Inland Revenue approval.

Employees are able to allocate part of their salary to acquire shares in the company that employs them, without paying tax or National Insurance. The employer is also exempt from National Insurance. Additionally, an employer can award free shares for participating employees.

There is a minimum deduction of £10 a month and a maximum of £1,500 a year, or 10 per cent of salary, if less.

The shares must be held for at least five years to benefit fully from the tax advantages.

Company share option schemes

An employer grants to an employee an option to purchase shares at a fixed price (which must not be discounted) at a future date. No income tax or National Insurance is payable on the granting of the option nor on any proceeds of sale, provided the option was taken out after 28 April 1996 and the total value of approved options did not exceed £30,000. There are additional rules for options taken out before this date and for options exercised more frequently than once every three years.

Approved profit-sharing schemes

An employer allocates shares to employees and places them in an approved trust. The maximum annual value for each employee is £3,000 or 10 per cent of their annual earnings (excluding benefits but after deducting pension contributions), whichever is the greater, subject to a ceiling of £8,000.

Provided you hold the shares for a minimum of two years, no income tax or National Insurance is payable on the allocation of the shares; nor on any profit when you sell the shares if held for at least three years.

However, no new schemes have been approved since 6 April 2001, and interest tax relief has not applied to shares given to employees since 31 December 2002.

Enterprise management incentives

Since 28 July 2000, small independent higher-risk trading companies have been able to reward up to 15 key employees with tax-advantaged share options, each employee receiving options worth up to £100,000 at the time of the grant.

Employment abroad (foreign earnings)

There are supplementary pages to the tax return which specifically deal with people who normally live in the UK but have income or earnings from overseas (see page 35).

There are measures which are intended to protect employees from double taxation in both the UK and the host country; principally the double taxation agreements held with various countries throughout the world.

If you receive a pension as a result of overseas employment, you will normally get a minimum of a 10 per cent deduction.

Before you take up an appointment abroad, be sure to check carefully, both with your employer and with your tax office, as to how foreign earnings in your particular instance will be treated for tax purposes.

Income from pensions and benefits

Under the Income section of the tax return (Q11) you have to state income you have received from the following pensions and social security benefits:

- State retirement pension.
- Widow's pension or bereavement allowance.
- Widowed mother's allowance or widowed parent's allowance.
- Industrial death benefit pension.
- Invalid care allowance and any taxable incapacity benefit.
- Jobseeker's allowance.
- Statutory sick pay and statutory maternity or paternity pay if it is not included in the P60 form given to you by your employer.

You also have to give details of other pension income you have received, including retirement annuities, and make a note of any tax deducted. If you have such pensions, it is important that you check how much tax you have paid at the end of each tax year to see if you are due a refund (see page 91).

CHAPTER 6

Your 2003 tax return
Claiming expenses against your income

There are certain types of expenditure which, if *necessary* for your job and provided at your expense, may be claimed against your income. Fill in the appropriate boxes in the expenses section of the Employment page of your tax return. To assist your claim it may be worthwhile to obtain a letter from your employer confirming that while your expenses are justified and necessary for your job, they are not reimbursed as a matter of policy.

It is important to keep a record of the details and dates on which the expenditure was incurred, and the bills where possible. Some allowable expenses are listed below.

Factory, manual and shop workers

- Extra costs incurred by employees working temporarily away from home, for example the cost of lunch if travelling away from the factory or office. Lorry drivers and construction site workers have special concessions.
- Overalls, boiler suits, boots, helmets, gloves and other special protective clothing. You should also include the cost of cleaning and repairing such items.
- Tools, toolbags and equipment.
- Travelling expenses (but see page 58).
- Trade journals and technical books essential to your job.
- Trade unions often agree with the tax inspector a fixed allowance which you can claim to cover certain expenses (e.g. engineers £45 to £120; agricultural workers £70). Alternatively, keep a record of all your expenses and submit an annual claim.

Healthcare workers

- A set of flat-rate expenses were introduced in 1998–1999. Your tax office will consider claims for the five years prior to the current tax year if you have not claimed expenses to which you were entitled.

Salesmen, office and clerical workers

- Travelling and hotel expenses on company business.
- Car expenses, with the exception of those relating to your private journeys. These should be claimed only after the deduction of any contributions made by your employer.
- If you use your own car for business travel, then you can claim the mileage allowances shown on page 50.
- Technical and other books on your firm's products or services. It may be advisable to obtain a letter from your employer confirming that this expenditure is necessary for your job.
- Use of your home as an office. If you are required to do a lot of work for your employer at home, and use a specific room for this purpose, you ought to claim an allowance based on a proportion of total upkeep, e.g. rent, light, heat, insurance, cleaning, repairs to furniture, etc. If such a room is used wholly for work a proportion of the council tax may be claimable, but some capital gains tax may be payable on the sale of the house. Such a claim should be made under the 'other expenses' box on the Employment sheet in your tax return. See also page 10.
- Telephone – part of your own telephone bill covering calls to customers, etc.
- Gifts to customers paid for by yourself which do not cost more than £50 per customer per year and which advertise your firm's products or services. (The gift must not be of food, drink, tobacco – or a voucher!)
- Fees, subscriptions, journals and publications essential to your employment or profession.

Travelling expenses

You are able to claim travelling expenses as a tax deduction against your income provided the journeys were not repetitive, i.e. from your home to a permanent place of work. This means that if your work takes you to many different locations, even if you start from home each day, then such expenses can be claimed. However, if you routinely visit a different office or branch each day of the week you may have more than one permanent workplace. The tax legislation is complicated, but where a site-based employee is working for more than 24 months at that workplace, it will be regarded as permanent and travelling expenses from home to site will not be allowed for tax.

Incidental overnight expenses

Miscellaneous personal expenses up to £5 a night paid by the employer whilst away from home on business in the UK (£10 a night abroad) are tax free.

Interest payments

If you have to borrow money to buy equipment (e.g. a computer) necessary for your job, then the interest can be claimed as an expense against your income. Relief for car loans has been withdrawn from 6 April 2002. Interest on a bank overdraft or credit cards is not allowable.

Employees earning £8,500 or more, and directors

All employees whose earnings, expenses *and potential benefits* are at the rate of £8,500 a year or more, and most directors regardless of their earnings or expenses, have their benefits and expenses reported to the tax office by their employer.

The employer has to do this by law and fills in the notoriously complicated form P11D, which is sent to the tax office. There is a legal obligation for all employers to give their employees copies of these forms by 6 July, which will be a help in checking your tax.

You might receive a letter from your tax office asking for details of these expenses, and you must then convince them that you did not receive any personal benefit or, if you did, obtain their agreement on the proportion of the expenses to be disallowed. You will pay tax on this proportion.

Sometimes an employer can arrange with the tax inspector to get a dispensation making it unnecessary for him or her to complete certain parts of form P11D, in which case the employee does not need to include such expense in the tax return.

The major conditions for a dispensation are normally that the reimbursement of expenses is closely supervised and it is obvious that the expenses themselves are easily justifiable (e.g. travelling and subsistence expenses for a representative).

Even if a dispensation is granted, the expenses still have to be taken into account in deciding if an employee earns £8,500 or more.

An employer may also make an arrangement to meet the tax liability on behalf of employees in respect of certain benefits. This is known as a PAYE Settlement Agreement and may cover items such as Christmas gifts, awards and shared benefits.

CHAPTER 7

Your 2003 tax return

Income from property and investments

This chapter deals with income from land and property, dividends and interest from investments, trusts and maintenance.

Assets held in joint names

If a husband and wife have income from an asset held in joint names, it is divided equally when filling in tax returns. If the ownership is not held equally, then you should ask the tax office for form 17 on which you can jointly declare the actual ownership split. You then enter the amounts accordingly in your tax returns. Such declaration takes effect from the date it is made, provided the form is sent to the tax office within 60 days.

Property income

The tax return supplementary pages Land and property cover all aspects of UK property income (see page 28).

If a husband and wife own a property that is let, the tax office will assume that any income from these assets is divided equally. You should enter in your tax return one half of the income and expenses, and tick the relevant box to indicate to the tax office that it is a joint holding. If the ownership is not held equally, then refer above as to the action you should take.

For the purposes of income tax, all income from property in the UK, including furnished, unfurnished and holiday lettings, is taxable on the same 'commercial' basis as any other business (see page 98) – that is, that expenditure is allowable against profits if it is wholly and exclusively for business purposes. Rent-a-room relief continues to be available, however.

To benefit from the furnished holiday letting tax rules, your property must be available for letting for at least 140 days in each tax year, actually let for a minimum of 70 days and not occupied for a continuous period of more than 31 days by the same person in any seven-month period (the tax laws are never straightforward!).

Property expenses

If you receive rents from a property which you let furnished or unfurnished you can claim the following expenses, if applicable:

- Rent paid and water rates.
- General maintenance and repairs of the property, garden and furniture and fittings.
- Costs of agents for letting and collecting rents.
- Insurance, including insurance premium tax.
- Interest payable on a loan to purchase, or improve, investment property (but see page 65 for restrictions).
- Charges for preparing inventories.
- Legal fees – on renewing a tenancy agreement, for leases of not more than 50 years, or on the initial grant of a lease not exceeding 21 years.
- Accountancy fees to prepare and agree your income.
- Costs of collecting rents, which could in some cases include your travelling expenses to and from the property.
- Costs of services e.g. porters, cleaners, security.
- Wear and tear allowance for furniture and fittings: generally 10 per cent of the basic rent receivable. As an alternative, the cost of renewals may be claimed.
- Council tax.

Rent-a-room relief

Owner occupiers and tenants who let furnished accommodation in their own or main home are able to receive rent up to £4,250 a year exempt from income tax. Make sure you tell your insurers and your mortgage company if you enter into a Rent-a-room arrangement.

If rent exceeds these limits, you have the option of either paying the excess without any deduction for allowable expenses, or calculating any profit made (gross rents less actual allowable expenses) and paying tax on that profit in the normal way.

An individual's exempt limit is halved if, at any time during a tax year, someone else received income from letting in the same property.

Interest from savings and investments

You need to differentiate between interest that has had tax deducted and that which has been paid gross.

If you have joint savings or investments include only your share of the income in the tax return.

Show all your income from National Savings, but exclude the first £70 interest earned on any ordinary account because this is tax free. You do not have to include interest from National Savings Certificates as that too is tax free.

Investment account interest is credited automatically to your account every 31 December – you can request a statement and the tax office will accept this figure to go on your tax return. You do not have to apportion it on a time basis.

Remember to include National Savings Capital Bonds under this section of the tax return. The interest is taxed on an annual basis, even though it is not actually received until the Bond is repaid after five years. Include details of First Option Bonds and Fixed Rate Savings Bonds separately.

There is no need to enter interest from SAYE accounts as it is not taxable.

Dividends from shares in UK companies

Enter the amounts that you actually received and the amount of tax credits as shown on your dividend slips. The date on the dividend slip is considered as being the date receivable for tax return purposes. Show income from most unit trusts here, including the income that was reinvested in further units instead of being paid direct to you. The treatment of tax credits is shown on page 82.

Scrip dividends should also be included here. The dividend statement should show 'the appropriate amount in cash', which is the dividend.

Accrued income securities

Where fixed-interest securities are sold or purchased and the contract note includes an adjustment for accrued interest, this will need to be reported on your tax return unless the nominal value of all your accrued income securities does not exceed £5,000 in the tax year concerned.

The rules are complicated, but the notes accompanying your tax return will include further guidance.

Income from trusts and settlements, etc.

Normally most estates of deceased persons will have a professional executor or administrator. They should provide you with a form R185, which will identify payments made to you and any tax deducted. If you do not receive this form, then seek advice as to the details you need to include in your tax return.

The tax return has supplementary pages covering Trusts and settlements (see page 32).

You may be able to claim tax back in respect of income from discretionary trusts (see page 84) if you are not a higher-rate taxpayer.

In the supplementary pages you also have to give details of settlements made, for although capital or income may not have been received by you, it may be considered by the tax office to be your income for tax purposes. The most common example would be income from gifts you may have made to minor children. (See also page 73.)

Children's income

If you have made gifts of capital to your children who are under the age of 18, the total income resulting from the gifts should be included in your tax return as savings income if it is in excess of £100 gross (but see also page 73).

Maintenance or alimony received

Since 6 April 2000, all maintenance receipts have been exempt from tax regardless of when the arrangement was made.

Prior to that, maintenance could be taxable if the legal arrangements were first made prior to 15 March 1988, and even then there was a maintenance exemption of £1,970.

CHAPTER 8

Your 2003 tax return

Interest and other payments allowed for tax

This chapter covers payments made by you which may be allowed for tax relief and should be shown on your tax return.

These could include interest charges on loans, covenants and donations to charities, maintenance payments, payments for vocational training, tax-efficient investments, and payments to trade unions and friendly societies.

Interest on loans for the purchase of private residence

Mortgage interest on loans to buy your own home was allowed for tax on loans up to £30,000 until 5 April 2000, the tax relief being restricted to 10 per cent.

The relief was completely withdrawn from April 2000.

Interest on loans to purchase an annuity

This relief was abolished for new loans taken out with effect from 9 March 1999.

For loans prior to that date, such interest continues to be allowed for tax if the person buying the annuity was aged 65 or over, the loan was secured on that individual's main residence in the UK or the Republic of Ireland and the loan did not exceed £30,000.

Tax at the basic rate can be deducted from the interest at the time of payment, provided the loan did not exceed this limit (see also page 94).

Interest on other loans

Having dealt with interest on loans for the purchase of property, there are other types of loans (called 'qualifying loans'), the interest on which is allowed for tax.

They include loans to buy shares or lend to:

1. A closely controlled trading company where you own more than 5 per cent of the company's shares or, if less, have worked for the greater part of your time in the management of the company.

Such interest is not allowed for tax if the shares qualified for tax relief under the Business Expansion Scheme or Enterprise Investment Scheme.

2. A partnership.

3. A co-operative, provided you work for it full time.

4. An employee-controlled trading company (share acquisition only).

Loans to pay inheritance tax or buy plant or machinery for business use also qualify (see page 40 – box 15.1).

Interest paid on loans to buy an investment property

Property investments are assessed on the same basis as any other business (see page 98) – that is, that expenditure is allowable against profits if it is wholly and exclusively for business purposes.

The interest rules also extend to overseas properties as well as those in the UK.

Refer to page 28 as to what has to be entered in the Land and property section of the return in box 15.2.

Retirement annuity payments and personal pensions

Refer to page 128 for a summary of the tax-efficient opportunities that can arise from pension planning.

Hire purchase and credit card interest

You cannot claim relief on this type of interest unless you pay it in connection with your business activities.

Interest on overdue tax

This cannot be claimed as a deduction for tax purposes.

Maintenance and alimony payments

You can now only get tax relief for maintenance and alimony payments if you, or your former husband or wife, were born before 6 April 1935 and you make legally enforceable payments. The maximum relief that can be claimed is the lower of the actual maintenance payments made or £2,150 (2002–2003 £2,110). Such relief ceases if your former husband or wife has remarried in 2002–2003.

Relief for all younger persons was abolished from 6 April 2000.

Venture Capital Trusts and Enterprise Investment Scheme

It is in the Reliefs section of your tax return (Q15) that you need to state details of the investments. See page 126 for tax advantages.

Giving to charities

The opportunities for giving to charities in a tax-efficient way have been considerably widened in the last couple of years.

The four main options are: payroll giving schemes; covenants; cash donations under a Gift Aid scheme; and gifting shares and securities.

Payroll giving schemes

Employers are allowed to run these schemes under which an employee can make donations to charity.

The donation is deducted from your pay and passed on to the charity by your employer. PAYE is calculated on your salary *after* making the deduction so that you are effectively getting immediate tax relief on the donation at your highest tax rate. Since 6 April 2000, there has been no minimum limit for donations.

There is no need to mention this in your tax return as you will have declared your net earnings in the Employment supplementary pages.

The Government adds a further 10 per cent to all such donations for four years from April 2000.

Covenants to charities

Covenants were used to transfer income in a tax-efficient way to charities; to be effective for income tax purposes they needed to be for more than three years.

You deducted tax from a payment under a deed of covenant at the basic rate and were able to claim higher-rate tax relief if applicable by claiming on your tax return.

Now that the Gift Aid scheme has been extended there will be no need for these types of covenant.

Gift Aid

This scheme applies to single gifts made by individuals and companies. Since 6 April 2000, there has been no minimum limit for donations. Gifts are regarded as being made net of basic-rate tax and charities are able to claim repayment of the tax. Relief is also available to non-residents who are liable to tax in the UK.

Higher-rate tax relief can be claimed where applicable by filling in the boxes in Q15A of your tax return.

Most charities have declaration forms for you to complete when you make a donation which will enable them to reclaim the tax.

If you do not pay tax, you should *not* use Gift Aid, otherwise you will eventually have to reimburse the tax office for the basic-rate tax deducted. The Inland Revenue publish a free booklet (IR65) on Giving to Charity. From April 2003, the tax return has been updated to remind taxpayers to claim Gift Aid and it will be possible to carry back relief to the previous tax year in certain circumstances. From April 2004, you will be able to nominate a charity to receive any tax refund due to you.

Gifts of shares, securities, land and buildings

Since 6 April 2000, quoted shares and securities can be gifted to charities and the full market value of the gift as well as the costs of transfer can be offset against your taxable income.

Similarly, from 6 April 2002, you can also gift land and buildings to charities (from 1 April 2002 for companies).

Individuals should enter the amount in boxes 15A.4 and 15A.5 of their tax return. There is no limit to the value of the gift, and in addition to income tax relief, the share sale or transfer to the charity will be free of capital gains tax.

Payments to trade unions and friendly societies

If you make compulsory payments to provide annuities for widows and orphans where relief is not given by your employer, or if part of your trade union subscription relates to a pension, insurance or funeral benefit, or you have a friendly society policy providing sickness and death benefits, then you can claim tax relief on one half of the payments.

Annuities and annual payments

If you made these payments for genuine commercial reasons in connection with your trade or profession, then box 15.9 of your tax return enables you to claim additional relief if you are a higher-rate taxpayer as they will have been treated as having been made after basic-rate tax has been deducted.

CHAPTER 9

Personal allowances and tax credits

A tax allowance is not a payment; it is the amount of income you can receive without paying tax. Apart from the personal allowance, all allowances are claimed by filling in a tax return.

The allowances for 2003–2004 as announced in the budget are as follows (for allowances for previous years see page 139).

Personal allowance	
Age as at 6 April 2003	£
Under 65	4,615
Between 65 and 74*	6,610
75 and over*	6,720
Notes	
*These age-related allowances are, however, restricted if your income is over £18,300. For every £2 of income above this limit, your allowance is reduced by £1, but no taxpayer can get less than the basic personal allowance of £4,615.	

The married couple's allowance

The married couple's allowance was abolished from 6 April 2000 except for couples where either the husband or wife was born before 6 April 1935 or where one person born before this date has married on or after 6 April 2000. The allowances for 2003–2004 are £5,565 (age between 65 and 74) and £5,635 for those aged 75 and over.

Relief is restricted to 10 per cent and the allowance is reduced, depending on your income level, by £1 for every £2 that your income exceeds the income limit of £18,300, but it cannot be reduced below the minimum amount of £2,150.

The personal allowance income restriction (see above) is applied before restricting the married couple's allowance.

A wife can claim one half of the married couple's allowance, or indeed the whole allowance, if her husband agrees. Ask your tax office for form 18, but this has to be submitted before the start of the tax year to which it relates.

If it is preferred that the husband gets the whole of the married couple's allowance then there is no need to take any action.

Blind person's allowance

A registered blind person is entitled to an extra tax allowance of £1,510 for 2003–2004 (£1,480 for 2002–2003). This is also claimable by blind persons in the year preceding the year in which they were officially registered blind if, at the end of the previous year, evidence was available to support the eventual registration. The allowance is transferable to a husband or wife even if he or she is not blind.

Tax credits generally

Over the past couple of years it has been Government policy to merge the tax system with the social security benefits system and to put less emphasis on tax allowances, making available tax credits instead.

Although the term 'tax credits' is somewhat misleading, it is intended that employers pay these to employees as part of the PAYE system; at least that was the theory, but the new child tax credit that came into force in April 2003 pays any benefit *directly* to the person caring for a child and *not* through the tax system. As with most recent tax legislation it is hopelessly confusing, and unnecessarily so.

There is a website to which you can refer for more information: www.inlandrevenue.gov.uk/taxcredits.

Child tax credit

This replaced the children's tax credit as from 6 April 2003. A claim form is available from any tax office or by telephoning 0800 500 2220. You can claim this credit if you have responsibility for caring for a child until 1 September following the child's 16th birthday (or 18th if the child is in full-time education). The amount you receive depends on the *joint* annual income of the parents or carers.

The Inland Revenue have a helpline on 0845 300 3900. They will also calculate any child tax credit due if you have more than three children.

Families with a new baby get a double payment for the first year.

Child tax credit rates						
Gross annual	*One child*		*Two children*		*Three children*	
joint income	*Annual*	*Weekly*	*Annual*	*Weekly*	*Annual*	*Weekly*
	£	£	£	£	£	£
Up to £10,000	1,990	38.00	3,435	65.70	4,880	93.30
£15,000	1,335	25.50	2,780	53.20	4,225	80.80
£20,000	545	10.40	930	17.80	2,375	45.40
£25,000–£58,000	545	10.40	545	10.40	545	10.40

There is a time limit of three months for backdating claims; therefore if payment is to commence from 6 April 2003, the claim needs to be made by 7 July 2003.

Child benefit, which is not means tested, is not affected by the introduction of this new tax credit.

Children's tax credit (up to 5 April 2003)

This tax credit of £5,200 started on 6 April 2001 but relief was only available at 10 per cent. It could be claimed:

- If you had a child living with you for at least part of the tax year.
- The child was aged under 16 at the start of the tax year.
- The child was your own (including a step-child or adopted child).

For couples, the person with the highest income had to claim, and provided neither of you paid tax at the highest rate of 40 per cent, you could elect for the parent with the least income to have all or an equal share of the allowance. If you paid tax at the higher rate, the allowance was reduced by £2 for every £3 of income taxed at the higher rate. You claimed the credit by filling in a form from your tax office or ringing a helpline on 0845 300 1036. If you have forgotten to claim this tax credit you can still do so and it will be backdated.

In addition, a 'new baby' rate of children's tax credit applied to a qualifying child between 6 April 2002 and 5 April 2003; the tax credit was £10,400 with relief being given at 10 per cent. The clawback provisions if you were a higher-rate taxpayer applied as above.

In your tax return for 2002–2003, fill in boxes 16.14 to 16.26.

Working tax credit

From April 2003, this replaced the working families' and disabled person's tax credits, the money for children in income support, income-based jobseeker's allowance and the new deal 50+ employment credit.

The working tax credit is a payment to top up the earnings of low-income workers. The amount you receive will depend on your income, hours worked, your age, and whether or not you have children. Unlike the child tax credit, the working tax credit will be paid through the PAYE system unless you are self-employed, in which case it will be paid directly to you. There are increased rates if you are disabled.

Additional sums may be claimable towards registered or approved child care ('the child care element within the working tax credit').

There is a helpline on 0845 300 3900.

Pension credit

Refer to page 88 for details.

CHAPTER 10

Family tax matters

W hether you are starting your first job, getting married, saving money or working on your own, you cannot escape the tax inspector.

Many people experience great difficulty in claiming repayments back from their tax office for one reason or another. The secret behind dealing with any tax claim is to comply with the system. The whole of our tax system revolves around filling in forms at the right time.

Either telephone your tax office, or call in or write and ask for the correct form, depending upon your circumstances. Fill it in and send it to your tax office in order to start the ball rolling. Always state your tax reference number. These days many of the forms are also available on the Inland Revenue website: www.inlandrevenue.gov.uk.

If you are taxed under PAYE, write to the tax inspector who deals with your employer's PAYE. If you are self-employed you will deal with the inspector who covers your business address.

Here are some practical steps to bear in mind.

Starting work

PAYE
You will need a code number (see page 77).

Your employer will fill in a form P46 and give this to you for signature. You then select which of the statements A, B or C applies to you, and complete the rest of the form.

If, however, you decide to work for yourself, or in partnership with someone else, you will eventually have to fill in a tax return on which you will claim your allowances and declare your income. Thus the PAYE system will not apply to you and all you need to do is to tell your tax office when your business commences (see page 96).

National Insurance contributions
National Insurance contributions are levied depending on how much you earn. See Chapter 15 for further details.

Changes in allowances and deductions

Most tax allowances and tax credits are not given to you automatically – they have to be claimed and the claim must be supported by the right information.

The more common instances of changes in allowances and credits are covered in this chapter.

Getting married

What should married couples do to benefit fully from the tax system?

1. **Personal allowances:** Both a husband and wife get a personal allowance in their own right; it will be wasted if neither work and have no income at all – it cannot be transferred from one to the other.

   To avoid one partner losing the personal allowance, consider transferring investments or savings so that the income can be offset against the husband's or wife's personal allowance.

2. **Married couple's allowance:** If you get married and either the husband or wife was born before 6 April 1935, then you can claim married couple's allowance for each month that you are married during the tax year and the full amount thereafter. Refer to page 68 to see if it is beneficial to transfer this allowance.

3. **Higher-rate tax:** If a husband or wife is paying tax at the higher rate (40 per cent), then transferring some income-producing assets between them would be beneficial if one partner is on the lower or basic-rate tax band, or is not using all of their personal allowance.

   Sometimes a husband or wife may be reluctant to transfer cash or assets in case they may be 'spent'. One solution is to transfer an asset into joint ownership as 'tenants in common'. Whilst the original owner could retain, say, a 95 per cent share, the Inland Revenue would treat the income as being split 50:50 if no declaration of actual ownership is made. In some cases it may be beneficial to make a declaration of ownership, in which case ask the tax office for form 17 *before* the start of a tax year (you cannot back-date such a request).

4. **Age allowances:** Married couples aged 65 and over should similarly check that their tax affairs are organised as above because both the higher personal allowance, which each of them gets in their own right, and the married couple's allowance, if applicable, are reduced if their incomes exceed certain limits (see page 89).

5. **Covenants:** Ensure that tax relief on covenants is not lost (see page 66).

6. **Capital gains:** If at all practicable, ensure that your investments are allocated between you or held in joint names so that you can each take full benefit of the capital gains exemption limit when investments are sold.

7. **Stakeholder pensions:** The new rules introduced from 6 April 2001 allow you to pay up to £3,600 a year into a pension fund even if you have no earnings. Consider setting up pension funds for a non-working husband or wife and/or children. These pensions are dealt with in more detail on page 129.

Raising a family

As soon as your baby is born, ask at your local benefits agency office for a child benefit claim form. Complete this and return it to them with the birth certificate.

Child benefit is normally payable to the mother, and collectable each week at the local post office or paid direct into her bank account each month. The benefit is tax free. Apply also for the child tax credit by telephoning 0800 500 2220 (see page 69).

Tax credits for families

Many of the tax allowances that previously helped families have been abolished and replaced by tax credits; details of all these are given in the previous chapter.

Childcare facilities

Employees can benefit from the use of childcare facilities provided by their employer without incurring a tax charge on that benefit.

To qualify for the exemption:

1. The child must be under 18.
2. The premises must not be domestic premises.
3. The premises must be provided by the employer (or a group of employers or a local authority) with each employer(s) being responsible for finance and management.
4. The care must be paid for directly by the employer (in other words, cash allowances, vouchers or reimbursement would not qualify).

There are no National Insurance contributions levied on childcare facilities provided by an employer.

Children's income

Each child is an individual taxpayer entitled to his or her own personal allowance. Parents are not taxable on a child's casual earnings nor on income arising on gifts from relatives. However, if you give cash or property to your children, the income will be treated as yours for income tax purposes if it exceeds £100 gross in the year.

In spite of the above, even if parents did give each of their children, say £1,400, then at say 6 per cent this would still be under the 'taxable limit' and the interest would be tax free.

Alternatively, consider Friendly Society Bonds. Take out a with-profits endowment bond to expire when the child is, say, 21 to build up a tax-free sum. The maximum premium allowed is £25 per month, and the maximum period is 25 years.

The only way in which parents can transfer larger sums to their children without continuing to pay tax on the income from those assets is by setting up an irrecoverable trust, which can accumulate income until the child is 18. However, if income is paid direct to the child before then, it will be taxed as the income of the parent.

On the other hand, a child can receive, or benefit from, income provided by a relative, either by the gift of investments or by setting up a trust which pays out income for the child's education and maintenance.

In these cases you should ask your tax office for form 232 on which to declare your child's income and, if the income has had tax deducted before receipt, for example trust income, interest, etc., claim a tax repayment in respect of the child's personal allowance.

Students
Earnings from holiday jobs will often have PAYE tax deducted. Ask your employer for form P38(S) which, when completed and returned, will enable payment to be made without tax deductions if the student does not earn above the personal allowance for the year.

Student loan repayments are now collected under the PAYE system once employment commences, and the employer has to deduct repayments depending on the income level. These 'contingent student loans' as they are called, have to be declared on your tax return.

One-parent families
In addition to the personal allowance, you should consider claiming the various tax credits as detailed in Chapter 9.

Divorce or separation
Inform the tax office of your changed circumstances. Obviously both parties keep their personal allowances and if you have been claiming married couple's allowance, then this will continue until the end of the tax year in which separation took place.

Any claim for children's or child tax credit may have to be reassessed depending on which partner looks after the children – or, indeed, apportioned if a child is to spend some time living with each partner (see page 69).

In the case of a woman who is paying National Insurance contributions at the reduced rate, then you should reconsider your position to see if you need to pay full-rate contributions to protect your benefits. (Ask for leaflet CA10, National Insurance contributions for divorced women, available from your tax office.

See page 65 for maintenance payments and page 131 for pension rights.

As regards the family home, if one partner sells, or gives it to the other within three years of the separation, there will be no capital gains tax payable; and still no tax will be payable if, after that period, one of the partners still resides there and the other partner has not claimed any other property as a main home.

Death of a wife or husband

Following the death of a husband where either spouse was born before 6 April 1935, a wife can claim any unused married couple's allowance.

After the death of a wife and provided the husband or wife was born before 6 April 1935, the husband will continue to get the married couple's allowance for that year (excluding any part that the wife may have used against her income) plus his own personal allowance.

A tax-free bereavement payment can also be claimed from the Department for Work and Pensions (DWP) by both widows and widowers subject to certain conditions.

Additionally, bereavement allowance and widowed parent's allowance might be available from the DWP, depending on your National Insurance status and contributions.

Ceasing employment

Permanently

Send parts 2 and 3 of form P45, which your employer will have given you, to your tax office; the district is shown on the form. Also write a letter confirming that you have either retired, ceased working or have become self-employed, and claim any tax repayment.

Temporarily

When you change employment or are made redundant and there is a gap between one job and the next, you will need to hand in form P45 when you sign on to claim benefits. The benefits agency will advise you on the proportion of your jobseeker's allowance that is taxable and will deal with any tax refund due at the end of the tax year. Alternatively, if you are not entitled to benefits, send in your P45 to your tax office telling them you are temporarily unemployed.

If you do not start a new job by the following 5 April, check your total income and tax, as shown in Chapter 12, to see if there is a repayment or underpayment of tax due.

Making a will

It is important to make a will. See page 120.

Are you claiming your tax refund?

There are broadly three main categories of people who should consider claiming tax refunds:

Savers with building society and bank accounts

Interest paid by building societies and banks will have had tax deducted from it at the savings rate (20 per cent) before it is paid to you.

If your total income is less than your personal allowance – as will often be the case for children, husbands or wives who are not earning and pensioners on low income – then you should claim that tax back.

Even if your total income does exceed your personal allowance, the starting rate of tax is only 10 per cent so you can claim the difference between the two rates.

Ask your bank or building society for form R85, fill it in and return it to them. Once they have this form, they can pay you interest in future without first deducting tax.

Pensioners

The above comments also apply to pensioners but, in addition, many pensioners whose income is less than their age-related allowance may also be receiving additional pensions and other interest on which tax has been deducted. Again, many will be entitled to tax refunds (see Chapter 12).

Shareholders

Many people, including children, who are not taxpayers because their income does not exceed their tax allowances, hold shares and receive dividends on which tax has been deducted in the form of a tax credit. You can make a claim up to five years from the 31 January deadline, although the tax credit cannot be reclaimed in these circumstances after 6 April 1999 and alternative investments that pay interest gross should be considered (see Chapter 18).

To claim a tax refund

Write to any tax office asking for leaflet IR110. This gives you some helpful information and, in particular, the leaflet contains a form for you to fill in and return to your tax office requesting a tax refund (see page 84 for further details).

CHAPTER 11

PAYE and code numbers

The Pay As You Earn system was introduced to enable every employee to pay tax by weekly or monthly instalments rather than in one hefty amount at the end of the tax year. By law, your employer has to deduct PAYE tax and NI from your earnings.

How does an employer know how much to deduct?

You are allocated a code number by your tax office, and that tells your employer how much you can earn before you start to pay tax. The code is a shortened method of defining your total tax-free pay (usually the total of your allowances), but in fact the last figure is omitted. The code effectively spreads your allowances evenly throughout the tax year. For example, a code 453L means that you start paying tax after you have earned £4,539 (£87.28 each week).

A notice of tax code is sent to you if your code changes; it details your allowances, benefits, untaxed income, etc., and shows your code number. If you do not receive one, you can request a copy from your tax office. You will need to quote your tax reference and National Insurance number.

Your employer is also advised of the new code but is not given the details as to how it is compiled *so he cannot check it for you.*

You should make sure that all allowances due to you are included and be sure your code is amended if your allowances alter during the year.

The higher your code, the lower your tax, unless you have a code with a K prefix.

What do the letters mean?

The letter shown after your code defines your status. For example, A = basic personal allowance plus 50 per cent of the children's tax credit, and a basic-rate taxpayer (H is used if you are to get all the children's tax credit); L = basic personal allowance; P = full personal allowance if aged 65–74 with V being used if you are also entitled to the married couple's allowance and you are on basic-rate tax; Y = personal allowance for those aged 75 or over.

OT means that no allowances have been given – that is often used if you haven't sent in a tax return for a long time or your tax affairs are very complicated. Other codes (BR, DO, T and NT) are sometimes used if you are working for more than one employer or have several sources of income.

Sometimes your taxable benefits will exceed your allowances – for example, if you are taxed on car and fuel benefits and private health benefits, or owe back tax. In these cases a K code is used so that your employer can recoup this tax on behalf of the tax office.

The tax office may *estimate* any likely taxable benefits for the 2003–2004 tax year and will probably base them on the latest available figures on their files, which could be quite old if you haven't sent in a tax return for the last couple of years.

You need to check the figures on your notice of code number carefully. If the estimates are excessive, write to your tax office requesting a code change – be sure to quote your NI number and the reference. If the estimates are much too low, bear in mind that if you take no action you may end up with a large underpayment at the end of the tax year.

How to check your code number

A typical notice of tax code will contain your name and address, tax office address, your tax reference number and your National Insurance number.

On the left-hand side will be your allowances. These will certainly include your personal allowance, to which may be added items such as the children's tax credit (up to 5 April 2003), married couple's allowance, allowable expenses, professional subscriptions, etc. If you are a higher-rate taxpayer, then any allowable payments on which only basic-rate tax has been deducted (e.g. personal pension payments, charity gift relief) will be shown here.

On the right-hand side will be the deductions, typically company car benefit, fuel benefit, other benefits and miscellaneous income on which you have not paid PAYE, and possibly an allowance restriction (see page 79). Any untaxed interest will be stated here. Any under or over payments of tax will relate to a previous tax year.

Deducting the right-hand column from the left-hand column will give you your net allowances; your code will be identified on the form.

On the reverse of the notice of tax code will be explanations showing when your new code will come into operation.

Ideally, the figures making up your code number should agree with the figures in your tax return.

If your code is incorrect, it is more than likely that your previous year's code was also wrong, so that any overpayment of tax is accumulating.

Pay particular attention to your company car and fuel benefits, as following the introduction of new rules, many coding notices have been issued showing incorrect benefits.

Pensioners will often have a code number applied to any supplementary pension they receive (see Chapter 13).

Allowance restriction

On the notice of code, any married couple's allowance or maintenance payments may be shown in full on the left-hand side even though the relief is only available at 10 per cent.

In order to adjust this, an allowance restriction will be shown on the right-hand side. There should be a calculation with your coding notice showing how this is made up. It is an extremely confusing and cumbersome way of restricting an allowance to 10 per cent.

Children's tax credit

This tax credit was renamed child tax credit from April 2003, and instead of being shown in your tax code it is now paid directly into the bank account of the person in the family mainly responsible for looking after the children. There is a telephone helpline on 0845 300 3900. See page 69 for further details.

CHAPTER 12

How to check your tax

At the end of the tax year you should check to see if you have paid the correct tax. Those who are self-employed may need to keep a closer eye on their tax affairs during the year and Chapter 14 specifically deals with this.

This chapter is primarily for employees on PAYE, although it will be of interest to all taxpayers as many of the circumstances are not confined to those on PAYE.

At the end of every tax year, your employer must give you a form P60, which will show how much you have earned in the tax year and, more importantly, how much tax you have paid.

If you receive benefits (company car, health insurance, etc.) you will also receive a form P11D (see page 59), which will identify these.

You should immediately check for yourself whether the amount of tax you have paid is correct. This will mean that you need to add up all your income and benefits, deducting allowable expenses (see Chapter 6) and any tax allowances, and calculating the tax payable.

If this total tax figure is less than that stated on your P60 form, then you have paid too much tax. Write immediately to your tax office pointing this out and then claim a refund. If you have not paid enough tax, either you or the tax inspector has made a mistake! If you have paid insufficient tax you are under a legal obligation to send in a tax return so that any outstanding tax can be calculated and paid. The tax office may also adjust your code number so that you do not underpay tax in the following year.

There is a comprehensive chart you can use in the *Check Your Tax* calculator on pages 133–135, but on the next few pages are simplified examples of how to check your own tax.

In the first example overleaf, Michael is a married man under 65 and the tax calculations are fairly straightforward, for he has no savings income or dividends and his income does not take him into the higher-rate tax band.

Assuming that these are the figures Michael declared in his 2003 tax return, then the statement he gets from the tax office should agree with his tax calculations and will also confirm that a refund is due. If he had adjustments in his tax code to collect underpayments for

Example 1: Checking your tax for the year ended 5 April 2003

Michael, who is married and under 65, is employed and had a salary of £27,300 from which his employer had deducted a pension contribution of £750. His employer provided him with a company car and fuel.

He did some freelance work at home which, after expenses, gave him £695. His tax liability can be summarised as follows:

	£	£
Total wages per P60 form	27,300.00	
Less: Pension contribution	750.00	26,550.00
Casual earnings		695.00
Use of company car and fuel benefit, say		5,500.00
Total earnings for the year		32,745.00
Less: Expenses claimed		115.00
Net earnings		32,630.00
Less: Personal allowance		4,615.00
Total income on which tax is payable		28,015.00
Tax payable £ 1,920 at 10 per cent	192.00	
£26,095 at 22 per cent	5,740.90	
Tax due		5,932.90
Less: Tax paid under PAYE as shown on form P60, say		6,114.00
Amount of tax to be claimed back		£ 181.10

earlier tax years, then these would need to be taken into the above calculation.

The tax office uses a different method

The way in which the above statement was prepared is the normal and simplest way, and the method most professional accountants would use. Unfortunately, our tax system always makes things as complicated as possible and the statements you receive from the tax office will present the details in a different format. They tend to work backwards, allocating income against tax bands.

However, the net result should be the same and if it is not and you cannot see at a glance why there is a difference, write to your tax office and enclose a copy of *your* workings so they can identify the problems.

Tax on savings income

Once the £1,920 income band at 10 per cent has been used, savings income (excluding dividends) is taxed at 20 per cent (not 22 per cent) if you are a basic-rate taxpayer; once your income takes you into the higher-rate band, then your savings are taxed at 40 per cent. Savings income is treated as the top slice of your income.

Tax on dividends

Just to complicate matters further, dividend income is paid after deducting a tax credit of 10 per cent. You have to add this tax credit to the amount of dividend received to give the gross amount to be included in your total income.

For basic-rate taxpayers this tax credit covers their tax liability on dividend income, but higher-rate taxpayers will be taxed at 32.5 per cent. Dividend income is treated as the top slice of your savings income.

This tax credit cannot be reclaimed if you are a non-taxpayer, although tax credits will be repayable until 5 April 2004 on shares held in Personal Equity Plans (PEPs) and Individual Savings Accounts (ISAs). Therefore choose investments that pay interest without tax having been deducted before you receive it (see page 92).

Checking your tax

As you will see, the tax system is unnecessarily complicated, but it can be made much simpler to understand if you remember to use the *Check Your Tax* sequence chart on page 83.

On the previous page it was explained how Michael, who had a fairly straightforward income structure without any savings income, calculated his tax.

Here are two more examples: Jane, who is a basic-rate taxpayer but has savings income and dividends; and Alan who is a higher-rate taxpayer with savings income and dividends and who also made a Gift Aid donation during the year.

Example 2: Checking your tax for the year ended 5 April 2003

In 2002–2003 Jane has a total income after allowances of £5,360 which includes £500 interest received gross.

She will pay tax on:

			£
The first	£1,920	at 10 per cent	192.00
	£2,940	at the basic rate of 22 per cent	646.80
	£ 500	at savings rate of 20 per cent	100.00
Total income	£5,360	Tax payable	£938.80

If Jane had received interest net after tax had been deducted, then the total income would still remain the same, for you must always include the *gross* amount of any income, but the amount of tax payable would be: £938.80 less £100 (20 per cent × £500) already deducted from the interest.

The Check Your Tax Sequence Chart

This is the easy way to calculate your tax. It is vital that you do your calculations in the following order:

1. Make a list of your total income under the following headings:

2. **Non savings income and benefits** (from which you deduct your allowances, expenses and pension payments): Taxed at 10 per cent up to £1,920, then at 22 per cent until the limit of the 22 per cent band is reached. Then at 40 per cent.

3. **Non-dividend savings income:** Taxed at 10 per cent if the £1,920 maximum has not been used up in the above calculation. Then at 20 per cent until the limit of the cumulative 22 per cent band is reached. Then at 40 per cent.

4. **Dividend income:** Taxed at 10 per cent until the limit of the cumulative 22 per cent band is reached. Then at 32.5 per cent.

Example 3: Checking your tax for the year ended 5 April 2003

Alan is married and under 65; he has a salary of £38,000, makes a pension contribution and receives benefits from his employer. He also has casual earnings, interest from a building society and dividends from shares. He also gave £500 to a local charity and signed a Gift Aid form so, that as a higher-rate taxpayer, he can claim the difference between the basic and higher-rate tax rate.

This is how Alan would go about checking his tax liability.

Alan lists his total income, less expenses and allowances, as follows:

	£	£
Total salary shown on his per P60 form	38,000.00	
Less: Pension contribution	3,800.00	34,200.00
Casual earnings		695.00
Use of company car and fuel benefit, say		5,500.00
Total earnings for the year		40,395.00
Less: Expenses claimed		115.00
Net earnings		40,280.00
Less: Personal allowance		4,615.00
Non-savings income		35,665.00
Non-dividend savings income received	432.00	
Tax deduced at 20 per cent	108.00	540.00
Dividend income received	450.00	
Tax credit	50.00	500.00
Total income		£36,705.00

As this total is above the maximum 22 per cent basic-rate band of £29,900, Alan is going to be a higher-rate taxpayer. Therefore apply the sequence in the box above to calculate his tax liability as follows.

	£		£
Tax on his non-savings income:	1,920.00 at 10 per cent		192.00
	27,980.00 at 22 per cent		6,155.60
Basic-rate band now reached	29,900.00		
£35,665–£29,900	5,765.00 at 40 per cent		2,306.00
Non-savings income total	35,665.00		
Tax on his non-dividend savings income:			
both the 10 per cent and 22 per cent bands have been fully used above therefore:	£540 at 40 per cent		216.00
Tax on his dividend income:			
both the 10 per cent and 22 per cent bands have been fully used above therefore:	£500 at 32.5 per cent		162.50
			£9,032.10
Less: Claim for Gift Aid donation	£500 at 18 per cent (40–22%)		90.00
			£8,942.10

Alan will already have paid much of this by PAYE deducted from his salary – let's say this was £8,500 – and has paid tax by deduction on his interest and dividend income.

So, Alan's final tax bill will be:

Tax liability as above		£8,942.10
Less: Paid under PAYE	£8,500.00	
Deducted from interest	108.00	
Tax credit on dividend	50.00	8,658.00
Further tax demand to pay		£ 284.10

Income tax repayment claim

If most of the income you receive has already been taxed (for example, interest) it is possible that you can claim back some tax.

Either fill in a self assessment tax return if you have received one or ask for a repayment claim form (form R40), telling your tax office in a covering letter that you think you are due a tax refund.

On form R40 you can claim expenses and deductions in the same way as an ordinary tax return. You do not have to send dividend vouchers and certificates of deduction of tax in support of your claim. However, you should still keep the records as you may be asked to produce evidence at a later date.

Do not forget, when you sign the declaration, that there is another part of the form that you need to sign, which is your legal request for the actual repayment of tax to be made to you.

Example 4: Tax repayment for the year 2002–2003

Joan, who is under 65, had a part-time job and earned £2,500, from which tax has not been deducted at source. She also received net interest from a building society of £2,000 (tax deducted £500).

	£	£
Earned income		2,500.00
Interest received	2,000.00	
Tax deducted (i.e. 20 per cent of £2,500)	500.00	2,500.00
Total income		5,000.00
Deduct personal allowance		4,615.00
		385.00
Tax liability: £385 at 10 per cent		38.50
Tax deducted at source		500.00
Tax refund due		£ 461.50

If Joan had received net *dividend* income of £2,000, instead of building society interest, she would not have been able to reclaim the tax credit that would have been deducted from her dividend.

Tax demands in respect of 2002–2003 income

If your only income is taxed under PAYE, then it is unlikely that you will receive a tax return to fill in and, provided you have checked that the right amount of tax had been deducted and your current PAYE code number is correct, then there is no need to contact your tax office.

If you have other income, or gains, in the year ended 5 April 2003 then you probably need to fill in a tax return. You should complete this and return it to your tax office before 30 September 2003.

The tax office will then send you a self assessment tax calculation (form SA 302) showing any sums due (or overpaid).

Should you wish to calculate your own tax, then you have until 31 January 2004 to send in the tax return *together with* payment of any tax due. However, you may be able to have any tax due collected through your tax coding if you submit your return by the earlier deadline of 30 September 2003.

Tax payments

Unless you are self-employed, or have sources of untaxed income, most of your tax liability will be paid by PAYE, or by deductions at source, throughout the year; when you send in your tax return, any tax due will be accounted for at the tax year end and is payable by 31 January of the following year.

If you are self-employed, however, or you have income or interest that has not been taxed, you will still have to make two payments on account – see page 46.

From time to time your tax office might send you self assessment statements (form SA 300) showing you the current position of your tax payments (or refunds). If it is correct, then any tax due must be paid by the date shown; if you disagree with the amount, ask for form SA 303 on which you can claim to reduce any payments on account, or write giving your explanation why you think the figures are wrong. You must still pay any tax that *you* think is due, however, otherwise interest will be charged.

Interest on late payments and repayments

The tax office will charge you interest on underpayments from the due date but will pay you interest – called a repayment supplement and which is not taxable – on overpayments. The interest rate for repayment supplements is generally 4.5 per cent lower than that charged on late payment (see page 46).

CHAPTER 13

Pensioners – your tax and your savings

This chapter applies only to those people who have reached the official retirement age of 65 for men and 60 for women. If you have elected for an earlier retirement you continue to be treated as a taxable individual and you cannot claim the tax concessions available to pensioners until the official retirement age. A married man is entitled to claim the retirement pension when he reaches 65. On the other hand, if a married woman reaches 60 before her husband is 65, she can only claim the pension if she has paid sufficient National Insurance contributions in her own right.

If the State pension is going to be your only income then you can apply to your local Department for Work and Pensions office and local council for various benefits to supplement your income; and also consider claiming tax credits and minimum income guarantee payments.

What to do when you retire

If you have been paying PAYE, you will receive a form P45 from your employer. Send this to the tax office printed on the form, with a letter stating that you have retired, giving the date on which you reached retirement age, details of any pensions you will receive, and stating that you are not intending to take further employment.

Should you later decide to work again, either full time or part time, you will have to ask your tax office for a new tax code.

If you have been self-employed, make sure that your tax returns are up to date and tax liabilities agreed, and inform your tax office of the details of any private pension you will receive.

Pensions

Most State pensions, including the old age pension, SERPS supplement and the widow's pension, are taxable, but the Government does not deduct the tax when you receive or collect them. If this State pension is your only source of income, however, then it is likely that no tax will be payable as your personal allowance will more than cover this income. The war widow's pension is not taxable, neither is the winter fuel payment or Christmas bonus.

Many people nowadays receive not only the State pension but also a pension from a former employer or an insurance company.

These additional pensions are normally taxed under PAYE and a code number is applied which will have taken into account the amount you receive from the State pension before calculating the tax due.

If you are receiving income from two or more sources, it may appear that your tax burden is out of all proportion to the income being taxed. This may be because the tax inspector is deducting from one source of income the tax in respect of *all* your income. Remember, that when the State pension increases, the tax on your other pension or income will go up as the State pension will eat into your tax-free allowance.

At the end of each tax year you should add up your total gross income and tax deducted to check how much tax you *should* have paid, as detailed in Chapter 12, in case any refund of tax is due to you.

SERPS and second State pension

The State earnings related pension scheme (SERPS) is a supplementary pension, earnings-related and varying according to how much you had contributed in full rate NI contributions. If you were 'contracted out' because you had an occupational pension scheme you will not be eligible for SERPS.

SERPS was replaced by a new State second pension from 6 April 2002, which gives proportionately more to low earners and carers. This will not affect any entitlement to SERPS that you have already built up.

Minimum income guarantee

This is designed to top up income where men and women over 60 have total income that is below £102.10 per week for single people and £155.80 for married couples. Total income is considered to include the State pension and any private pension and certain social security benefits. Like all recent tax and social security legislation it is complicated, but if you are on low income you should apply for what is rightfully yours – there is a helpline on 0800 028 1111.

You cannot qualify for the full amount if you have assets over £10,000 (£16,000 if you are in residential care or a nursing home).

Pension credit

From October 2003 there will be a new pension credit to top up pensioners' income, whilst at the same time rewarding those who had saved for their retirement. See Appendix 2 on page 137.

It will depend on your total income and savings (so it is therefore means-tested) and will help single people aged 65 or over with an annual income up to £7,219 or a couple with an income up to £10,584. The Government will announce later in the year the procedure for claiming this credit – one thing is certain, and that is the arithmetic will be complex, which will deter a lot of pensioners from claiming.

Note also other tax credits listed in Chapter 9.

Working after retirement

If you carry on working after the official retirement age (65 or 60) you can still claim the State pension, although you do not have to pay any more National Insurance contributions (employers still have to contribute, however).

Whether you are employed full time or part time, a PAYE code will be issued (see page 77) that will tax your earnings.

Tax allowances

A husband and wife each have their own tax allowance and are responsible for their own tax affairs.

The tax allowances for 2003–2004 are as follows with the 2002–2003 figures in brackets:

Tax allowances for 2003–2004		
Age for personal allowance	Personal allowance £	Married couple's allowance £
65–74	6,610 (6,100)	5,565 (5,465)
75 and over	6,720 (6,370)	5,635 (5,535)

Notes
Although the married couple's allowance was abolished from 6 April 2000, it still continues for those couples where either the husband or wife was aged 65 or more on or before 5 April 2000 and is based on the age of the *older* of the husband or wife. Relief is restricted to only 10 per cent of the allowance.

However, these age-related personal allowances, as they are called, are reduced if your own total income is above £18,300 (£17,900 for 2002–2003). For every £2 of income above this limit, your allowance is reduced by £1, but no taxpayer can get less than the basic personal allowance of £4,615 (£4,615 also for 2002–2003). Similarly, the married couple's allowance will also be reduced by the excess that has not already been taken into account in calculating the reduced personal allowance. Once again, the allowance cannot be reduced below the minimum level of £2,150 for 2003–2004 (£2,110 for 2002–2003).

Don't forget that a wife's income from all sources is considered separately from that of her husband.

How to check your tax for 2002–2003

Start by finding out your total income for the year. You must include all your pension income, *including* the State pension and the *gross* amount of any interest from banks, building societies, annuities, etc. Also include any dividend income, including the tax credit. You do not have to include any income that is free of tax (see page 9).

Secondly, you need to make a note of any tax that you have already had deducted from your pension or other income. Finally you need to calculate any allowances to which you are entitled.

Remember that if a situation arises where a husband is unable to use part of his married couple's allowance, the balance can be transferred to his wife – ask for Form 575 from your tax office. You have up to five years from 31 January following the tax year in which to make this request.

Example of how to check your tax for 2002–2003			
John, the husband, is aged 73 and his wife, Mary, is 69.		John £	Mary £
Income for 2002–2003			
State pension, say		3,926.00	2,350.00
Other pension, gross amount (tax deducted, say £1,400)		8,886.00	
Rent from letting unfurnished room (after expenses)		4,046.00	
Income before interest and dividends		16,858.00	2,350.00
National Saving Bank interest:			
Ordinary account £40 (the first £70 is not taxable)		–	
Investment account (gross)		–	75.00
Bank deposit interest – received	£ 144.00		
Tax deducted before receipt	36.00	180.00	
Dividend income – received	1,800.00		
tax credit	200.00	2,000.00	
Total income		19,038.00	2,425.00
Less: Personal allowance	6,100.00		6,100.00
but restricted because of John's income limit (see note) £19,038–£17,900 = £1,138 × 50 per cent	569.00	5,531.00	(3,675.00) unused allowance
Taxable income		£13,507.00	

Now refer to the sequence chart on page 83 so that you use the correct percentages in calculating your tax.

		£
John's tax liability will be:		
On his non-savings income £16,858		
Less: his allowances £ 5,531 = £11,327		
	£1,920.00 at 10 per cent	192.00
	£9,407.00 at 22 per cent	2,069.54
On his savings income	£180 at 20 per cent	36.00
On his dividend income	£2,000 at 10 per cent	200.00
		2,497.54
Less: married couple's allowance £5,465 at 10 per cent		546.50
Total tax liability		1,951.04
But he has already paid by deduction the following amounts of tax:		
On his other pension	£1,400.00	
On his bank interest	36.00	
On his dividends	200.00	1,636.00
Tax still to pay		£ 315.04

Notes
1. John's total income was £19,038; as the income age limit is £17,900 his allowances are reduced by 50 per cent (£1 for every £2 over this limit). This could have been avoided if some of his income-producing assets had been transferred to Mary, his wife.
2. It will be seen that Mary had insufficient income to cover her personal allowance. The unused balance is lost – it cannot be used by her husband. It would have been more sensible for her to have received a greater part of the family income in order to reduce John's tax liability, so they should consider reorganising their investments to avoid the same problem arising next year.
3. Perhaps John should also have let the room furnished instead of unfurnished, with the lodger sharing the house so that the rent could have been received tax-free under the rent-a-room scheme (see page 61).

If John and Mary were working out their likely tax situation for 2003–2004 they would still get the married couple's allowance (increased to £5,565). The age income limit would be £18,300 and the basic rate of tax stays the same at 22 per cent.

It will still be important that John transfers some income-bearing investments to his wife, but she should not receive dividends as she cannot reclaim the tax credit if her income remains below her personal allowance; investments paying interest tax free would be preferable (see below).

Income tax repayment

At the end of each tax year on 5 April you should check to see exactly what income you received during the year and what tax you have actually paid, as in the above example.

You can get a repayment of tax if you have paid too much. To reclaim tax ask your tax office for leaflet IR110 and a form R40.

Complete it in the same way as a tax return (see Chapter 4) and send the form to your tax office. There is no need to enclose the dividend and interest vouchers unless the tax office ask for them at a later date.

Where most of your income has already had tax deducted before you receive it (for example, interest) you may be able to make quarterly, half-yearly or annual repayment claims (see page 84).

Even if you *are* a taxpayer, you may have had tax deducted from interest received at 20 per cent and because you haven't had the benefit of the 10 per cent tax band (see page 139) you should claim a refund of the difference. There are a great number of pensioners on low incomes who are not making these claims.

Where to invest your money

In reviewing investments, married pensioners in particular should make sure that they are making full use of both personal allowances.

They should avoid a situation arising where perhaps a husband or his wife is paying tax and either of them is not using their full allowances. To correct such a problem, you should consider switching savings or investments from one to the other.

If you have insufficient income to cover your personal allowances (that is, you are not a taxpayer) it is important to put your savings into investments that pay interest gross. Consider the following:

Building society and bank accounts

These accounts will pay interest without tax being deducted provided you fill in form R85 and give the completed form to your bank or building society branch. On this form you have to certify that your total income for the tax year is unlikely to exceed your personal allowances. If you are aged 65 to 74 on 5 April 2003 these figures for 2003–2004 are £7,166 for a married man and £6,610 for anyone else; if you are 75 or more they are £7,283 for a married man and £6,720 for anyone else (assuming an election has not been made to transfer all or part of the married couple's allowance).

You will need your National Insurance number to complete this form. If your circumstances change during the tax year and your total income is such that you will become liable to tax, you must inform your bank or building society branch immediately.

If you do not complete form R85, then tax at the savings rate will be deducted from your interest payments, and if you are not liable to tax you will have to wait until the following April before claiming any tax back from the tax office. However, if your repayment claim is for £50 or more, then you can apply for a refund at any time during the tax year – ask your tax office for leaflet IR110.

National Savings Bonds
Income bonds: These are designed for those who wish to receive regular monthly payments of interest while preserving the full cash value of their investment. Interest is paid monthly without tax being deducted, and should be declared on your tax return.

Capital bonds and fixed rate bonds: These are similar but gross interest is added to the capital value annually – they must be declared on your tax return.

National Savings bank accounts
All interest is paid gross and must be included in your total income for tax purposes except for the first £70 of interest on an ordinary account. The investment account pays a higher interest rate than an ordinary account.

Pensioners' Guaranteed Income Bonds
These are bonds carrying a fixed rate of interest for five years but you can also consider one-year and two-year bonds. They are specifically for people over 60 years of age. Bondholders must have a bank, building society or National Savings investment account to which interest can be transferred automatically. To obtain early repayment, 60 days notice is required with a corresponding loss of income.

As with all fixed-interest investments you have to be confident that the market interest rates are not going to increase materially over the next few years.

Remember to keep an eye on the maturity date. The National Savings office will write to you, but if you don't respond within a couple of weeks they will re-invest your capital in a similar dated bond and you will lose your option to consider other selections.

Government stocks
You can no longer purchase or sell gilt-edged securities at the post office. Instead, ask for a form from the Bank of England Registrar on freephone 0800 818 614. The interest on Government Stocks is paid to you regularly without deducting tax, unless you request that it should be paid net. No capital gains tax liability arises on any profit when you sell but the interest should be declared on your tax return.

With all the above investments you should declare the interest in your tax return in the event of your total income (including pensions) exceeding your total allowances, for you will be liable to tax on the difference.

Where to invest if you are a taxpayer

If your income is sufficient to cover your allowances, then in addition to the above, you should consider:

Index-linked National Savings Certificates

You receive no interest but if held for at least a year your capital is inflation-proofed and, with annual supplements expanded to 3 per cent compound interest over a five-year period, this 'profit' is exempt from income tax and capital gains tax.

Fixed-interest National Savings Certificates

Interest is added throughout the five-year life of the certificate and is free of income tax. You sacrifice some interest if you cash them before the expiry date. The interest does not have to be entered on your tax return.

Bear in mind with the above investments, that you will not get the full benefit of the investment returns if you do not hold the certificates for the full five years.

National Savings have a telephone enquiry line on 0845 964 5000 and a website: www.nationalsavings.co.uk.

Chapter 18 gives more investment ideas, including individual savings accounts (ISAs).

Annuities and home income schemes

To improve your standard of living and to increase your spendable income you could mortgage your house to an insurance company and use the lump sum to buy an annuity.

When you receive an annuity payment it consists of two elements: capital and income. The capital portion is non-taxable but the insurance company will deduct tax from the income portion (which you must enter on your tax return) and provide you with a tax deduction certificate, which you will need in order to claim any tax repayment. Tax will be deducted at the basic rate of 22 per cent.

You will not get any tax relief on buying the actual annuity. However, provided at least 90 per cent of the lump sum received on mortgaging your house was used to buy the annuity and the loan was taken out before 9 March 1999, then the interest on a mortgage of up to £30,000 will be tax deductible at the basic rate, even though mortgage interest tax relief was abolished for other loans from 6 April 2000. You had to be 65 or over at 9 March 1999.

Annuities are particularly useful if you have no dependants or your children or relatives do not need additional assets.

Bear in mind that any extra income from an annuity could reduce any means-tested social security benefit, could affect your age-related personal allowance and will not take inflation into account in succeeding years. Also, you cannot cancel an annuity and get your capital back.

Your pension scheme retirement options

If you are a member of your employer's pension scheme or have a personal pension scheme of your own, it is important to consider all of the options when you retire.

On your retirement, a tax-free cash lump sum payment is normally available, the calculation of which depends on the type of scheme.

If you are a member of your employer's final salary occupational pension scheme, your lump-sum calculation will depend on your years of service and taxable earnings (including P11D benefits) at retirement. You should ask your insurance company or scheme administrator for this information; money purchase schemes have different rules.

If you have your own personal pension plan or retirement annuity, then broadly the tax-free cash lump sum is equivalent to 25 per cent of the total accrued fund available.

The balance of your fund must be used to provide an income which can be paid in one of two ways:

- *Either* via an annuity purchased from an insurance company – ask several companies for a quotation taking account of your own circumstances. You do not have to stay with the insurance company with whom you have had the pension scheme. When getting quotes there will be several options, e.g. do you wish to include a pension for your husband or wife? Does your own contract have a guaranteed annuity rate written into the plan since these may be better than those available in the marketplace?

- *Or* by drawing down the income from the fund, known as 'income drawdown'. This facility is only available up to age 75 to those who hold a personal pension. If, therefore, you are a member of a company scheme or retirement annuity you will need to transfer all the accrued fund into a personal pension plan before drawing any tax-free cash.

  Until an annuity is purchased, an income can be drawn from the pension fund equivalent to between 35 per cent and 100 per cent of the highest annuity that the fund could have purchased.

This is an extremely complicated area and you should seek specialist independent advice if you wish to investigate these options.

CHAPTER 14

Self-employed

A self-employed person is one who owns a business or is in partnership with someone else. If you trade as a limited company, you, as a director, are an employee and not self-employed.

Advantages over PAYE

Self-employed people do not pay PAYE – this method of collecting tax is strictly for employees; instead they pay tax on their profits under what is called Schedule D.

There are definite advantages in paying tax under Schedule D as there are more opportunities for self-employed people to reduce their tax bill than an employed person. There are more expenses that can be claimed and they are somewhat easier to claim. In addition, there is loss relief which can be set against other taxable income or, in the early years of a business, can be carried back against your total income for the previous three years.

If you are self-employed, you may find it more convenient to deal with the paperwork and meet some of your business contacts at your home. This, in effect, becomes a second place of business, so that you can claim against your profits a proportion of the expenses, such as heating and lighting.

Start off on the right lines

1. When you start a new business, you must tell you tax office within three months of starting, otherwise you could face a fine of £100.

    You also need to notify the NI contributions office so that you don't build up arrears of NI contributions or miss out on benefits. The Inland Revenue issues a booklet *Starting Your Own Business* CWL1, which has useful advice and a form which can be used to notify the relevant departments of your new business.

2. You might have a tax liability in the first year, unless you make a loss or your profit is offset by allowances or reliefs. Do not wait for the tax office to send you a tax return – ask for one.

3. You may have been employed before starting up in business on your own. If so, you should send the P45 form you will have

received from your previous employer to your local tax office and you may be able to claim a tax refund immediately.

4. If you do not use your own name you must show the names and addresses of the owners of the business on business letters, orders, invoices, receipts and demands for payment. You must also display the names and addresses at your business premises.

5. It may be advantageous to take your wife or husband in as a partner if not already employed elsewhere. Do not forget that, depending on earnings levels and share of profits, there might be a liability to pay tax and National Insurance contributions (see page 106).

6. When you are in a partnership it is advisable to have a written agreement setting out its terms, particularly if your wife or husband is a partner.

7. You should open a separate bank account for your business which, in the case of a partnership, should be in the partnership names.

8. Keep books detailing your business dealings: the minimum you should keep are a cash book for all monies received and paid, an analysis book for purchases and one for sales, and a petty cash book for miscellaneous expenses.

   It is essential that you keep all purchase invoices and copy sales invoices, not only for the purpose of preparing your accounts but also to keep a check on the amounts you may have to pay and charge in respect of value added tax.

   Check your turnover – should you register for VAT (see page 139)?

9. Always bear in mind that both the tax inspector and the VAT inspector have a legal right to require you to supply evidence from your books and records for any particular year. *Under self assessment you must keep books and records for five years and ten months from the end of the tax year.*

10. Make regular provision for a retirement pension – see page 128.

11. Check your insurances – advise your insurers if you are operating from your home address or using your own car.

12. Since 6 April 2001, it has been possible to establish limited liability partnerships (LLPs), the main purpose of which is to protect partners from excessive claims against the partnership.

How are you taxed?

Many self-employed people think you pay tax only on what you take out of the business for yourself as drawings or wages. This is not so. Drawings are sums taken on account of the profit you expect to make. You are taxed on your total profit before deducting any drawings.

To find out how much profit you have made, prepare an account showing your total business income less your business expenses. This is not necessarily the figure on which your tax is calculated, for you have to add any disallowable items mentioned below.

It is this amended profit figure, not the one shown in your accounts, that you should enter in your tax return. Your claim for capital allowances must also be entered (see page 102). This adjustment and claim for capital allowances is called a tax computation.

Allowable expenses and deductions

Apart from your normal business expenses (e.g. purchase of goods, rent, rates, staff wages) you should consider claiming the following:

- Hotel and travelling expenses on business trips – not forgetting part of the total running expenses of your car.
- The business usage part of your private telephone bill.
- Bank interest and charges on your business account.
- Business subscriptions and magazines.
- Special clothing necessary for your type of business, including cleaning costs, etc.
- Bad and doubtful debts which can be specifically identified.
- Gifts advertising your business (but the cost must not exceed £50 per person, and not be food, drinks, tobacco or vouchers).
- Repairs and renewals to business property (e.g. the cost of replacing a shopfront, less any part of that cost representing any improvement).
- Employer's National Insurance contributions on employee's wages and benefits (see page 108 for your own NIC deductions).

Expenses and deductions not allowable

It is possible that your business payments include some expenses which are not allowable for tax. In this case, your profit must be increased so as to exclude this private element. Examples of the more usual items are a proportion of:

- Rent, light, heat and council tax – where you live in part of the business premises (e.g. a flat above your shop).
- Motor car expenses, including hire purchase interest, where you use a business car for private journeys.

- Telephone bills.

And the whole of:

- Depreciation on all assets, if included in your accounts, whether they are business or private. You can instead claim capital allowances (see page 102).
- Capital expenditure – the cost of computers, cars, machinery, etc., or expenditure involving improvement as distinct from the repair of an asset. Claim capital allowances instead.
- Entertaining either UK or foreign customers.
- Your own earnings.
- Class 2 and Class 4 NICs (see page 108).
- Donations to political parties.

Example of business accounts and a tax computation
It has been assumed that Mr Wiltshire has been in business for several years, as there are special rules for new businesses.

John Wiltshire – Florists
Profit and Loss Account for year ended 5 April 2003

	£		£
Opening stock	750	Sales or takings	77,000
Purchases	22,000	Closing stock	2,500
Gross profit	56,750		
	£79,500		£79,500
Staff wages and NIC	6,842	Gross profit	56,750
Rent and rates	14,126	Rent receivable	750
Telephone	427	Profit on sale of	
Light and heat	623	motor car	398
Legal fees re new lease	100	Interest received (gross)	105
Insurance of shop	181		
Motor expenses	512		
Travelling/entertaining	107		
Postage and stationery	87		
General expenses	202		
Bank charges and interest	64		
Depreciation:			
Motor car	600		
Fixtures	376		
Repairs and renewals	789		
Wife's wages	980		
Own wages	20,000		
Own NIC	278		
	46,294		
Net profit	11,709		
	£58,003		£58,003

Although Mr Wiltshire will start with these accounts, various adjustments will have to be made to arrive at an adjusted profit for tax purposes. A tax computation based on the accounts will have to be prepared as follows:

John Wiltshire – Florists
Profit adjusted for income tax for year ended 5 April 2003

	£	£
Profit per accounts		11,709
Less: Income taxed separately:		
Rent received	750	
Interest received gross	105	
Profit on sale of motor car	398	
		1,253
		10,456
Add: Items not allowable for tax purposes:		
Own wages and NIC	20,278	
Repairs and renewals – new till	525	
Depreciation: Motor car	600	
Fixtures	376	
General expenses – political donations	22	
Entertaining customers	66	
Motor expenses – 20 per cent private use	102	
Legal fees re new lease	100	
		22,069
		32,525
Less: Capital allowances	1,100	
Less: Private use of car £ 220		
Balancing charge re motor car 144		
	364	
		736
Taxable profit		£ 31,789

Mr Wiltshire's tax liability is as follows for 2002–2003:

	£	£
Taxable profit (as above)		£ 31,789
Deduct: Personal pension (note 1)		1,820
		29,969
Rent	750	
Interest	105	855
		30,824
Deduct: Personal allowance		4,615
Taxable income		£ 26,209
Total income tax payable		
£ 1,920 at 10 per cent		192.00
£ 105 at 20 per cent (savings)		21.00
£24,184 at 22 per cent		5,320.48
£26,209		5,533.48
Add tax relief at source on pension contributions (note 2)		400.40
Class 4 NIC payable: £30,420 (max) – £4,615		
(lower limit) at 7 per cent		1,806.35
Total tax and NIC		£ 7,740.23

Notes

1. Mr Wiltshire paid only £1,820 to a personal pension plan; he could have paid up to £5,563 (17.5 per cent of £31,789), assuming he is under 35, as the maximum allowed (see page 130).

2. Since 6 April 2001, all contributions to personal pension plans are payable net of basic rate tax.

3. If Mrs Wiltshire's wages are going to be her only income next year, she will lose part of her own personal allowance if they stay at their current low level. It would be more tax advantageous to increase her wages to utilise her full allowance and thus reduce the tax paid by Mr Wiltshire on his profits.

4. Mr Wiltshire will make payments on account of his tax and NIC liability on 31 January and 31 July 2003, paying (or receiving) any balance on 31 January 2004.

Pension contributions

Refer to page 130 for self-employed pensions.

Simplified accounts

If your turnover is less than £15,000, the self assessment tax return gives you the option of just filling in boxes for your turnover figure, expenses total and net profit, although you will obviously need to compile accounts for your own use to arrive at the figures, and you must keep all documentation in case the tax office raises queries.

Capital allowances

You should set aside part of your profits to save for the replacement of those assets which either become worn out or obsolete. This provision would be shown as depreciation in your accounts.

As mentioned in the previous section, your depreciation provisions are ignored for tax purposes and instead you can claim capital allowances (see table overleaf) as a tax deduction.

Special apportionment rules apply when a business begins or ceases.

Remember that you can claim capital allowances on assets that you transfer to the business when you start up (e.g. furniture, car, etc.).

If you use a business asset for private purposes – for instance, a motor car for the weekends and holidays – you must reduce the allowances by the proportion representing your private use.

If one year's business profit was small enough to be covered by your tax allowances, or you had suffered a trading loss so that you pay no tax, then it may be more worthwhile for you not to claim the whole of the capital allowances; this would keep the written down value for tax purposes higher to give you larger writing down allowances to set against your future profits.

Buying plant and machinery

It is normally better to buy plant or equipment on the last day of one financial year rather than the first day of your next year – the reason being that you get the equivalent of a full year's capital allowance even though you have owned it for only a matter of hours and, although legally yours, have not necessarily paid for it. You need not pay the whole purchase price, but can buy on hire purchase.

Table of capital allowances

	First year capital allowance	Writing down percentage on reducing balance thereafter
From 2 July 1998		
	per cent	per cent
Plant, machinery and equipment*	40†	25
Fixtures and fittings	40†	25
Motor cars (maximum £3,000 a year)	–	25
Vans and lorries	40†	25
Office furniture and equipment	40†	25
Insulation of factories and warehouses	40†	25
Fire safety expenditure	40†	25
From 1 April 2000 to 31 March 2004		
Computer hardware and software, high-tech, mobile phones and internet set-top boxes (For small businesses only)‡	100	–
From April 2001		
Creating flats over shops for letting	100	–
Energy saving plant and machinery	100	–
For details of eligible equipment telephone helpline 0800 585 794		
From 17 April 2002		
Low-emission or electric cars (new)	100	–
		on cost
Factories and warehouses	–	4
Agricultural buildings	–	4
Hotel buildings	–	4
Houses under assured tenancies scheme	–	4

Notes
* The annual rate of writing down allowance will be reduced to 6 per cent for most assets with a working life of 25 years or more purchased, or contracted, on or after 26 November 1996, but this applies only to businesses which spend more than £100,000 a year on such assets.
† Only applies to small to medium-sized businesses (see below). There are higher rates for Northern Ireland.
‡ Small businesses are defined as having an annual turnover of not more than £2.8 million, assets not exceeding £1.4 million with a maximum of 50 employees. (The figures for medium-sized businesses are £11.2 million, £5.6 million and 250 employees respectively.) Two out of three conditions must be met.
1. There are higher allowances for buildings in enterprise zones, scientific research and film production expenditure, and special provisions for patent rights, know how, mines, mineral rights and certain other assets; also 150 per cent tax credits from 1 April 2000 for research and development.

Selling plant and machinery

All plant and machinery with a 25 per cent writing down allowance (other than cars and other assets with an element of private use) is 'pooled' and on any sale you only have to deduct any proceeds of sale before calculating the writing down allowance.

If the proceeds exceed the total value of the pool, after adding the additions for the year, the excess will be charged to tax as a balancing charge. On cars costing £12,000 or more, the maximum allowance is £3,000 a year. Assets used in part privately also have to be grouped in separate pools.

With any other asset acquired on or after 1 April 1986, if you expect to dispose of it within two years for less than the tax written down value, you can elect within two years of the year of acquisition to 'depool' the asset. On disposal, the difference between the tax written down value at that date and the proceeds, if less, will be allowed as an extra relief (known as a balancing allowance) or, if more, charged to tax as a balancing charge.

Your tax assessments

For existing businesses

Profits are assessed to tax based on the accounts year ending during the tax year; for example, accounts made up for the year ended 30 June 2002 would be the basis for the 2002–2003 computation, those made up to 5 April 2002 would be for 2001–2002.

For new businesses

The date to which you prepare accounts is entirely up to you. Special rules of assessment apply for the first two tax years. For example, if your first accounts are for year ended 30 June 2002, your tax computations will be based as follows:

1. Year one 2001–2002: On the profit earned between the 1 July 2001 starting date and 5 April 2002 (apportioned on a time basis).
2. Year two 2002–2003: On the profit earned for the first 12 months of trading (i.e. year ended 30 June 2002.)
3. Year three 2003–2004: On the accounts for the year ended 30 June 2003.

As you will see in the above example, part of the first year's profits are taxed twice in years one and two (1 July 2001 to 5 April 2002). This is referred to as the overlap profit and details should be kept of the overlapping period and profit, as you are able to claim overlap relief if your business ceases or, in certain circumstances, you change the date to which you draw up your accounts.

Your tax bills

You pay tax on your adjusted profit less capital allowances, personal allowances and deductions you will have claimed in your tax return.

Your total tax bill is normally payable by two equal instalments on 31 January and 31 July in each year, to which is added any Class 4 National Insurance contributions (see page 108).

If you are in a partnership, the partnership profits will still need to be agreed in the firm's name and no partner can independently agree just his or her own share of the profits. However, the tax liability for each partner will be calculated separately, taking into account each partner's personal allowances and reliefs. Partners are no longer responsible for the other partners' tax liabilities.

Trading losses

If you should make a loss it can be deducted from:

1. Other income, and then any capital gains, of the same tax year.
2. Other income, and then any capital gains, of the previous year.
3. Trading profits of future years.
4. Any income in the preceding three tax years, provided the loss arises in the first four tax years of a business, but note that losses are set against the earliest years first.
5. Any profits over the previous three tax years if the loss arises in the last 12 months before closing down.

Deductions are made in the order that saves most tax.

You cannot claim all your tax reliefs and only a part of the loss; you must claim the whole of the loss first. Therefore before making a claim for loss relief, you should calculate whether you would lose a significant proportion of your personal allowances and deductions.

If, after deducting the loss as suggested above, you find that the remaining income is insufficient to cover your personal allowances, it may be better to carry forward the whole loss with a view to setting it off against future profits from the same trade.

National Insurance contributions

Another liability you have while you are running your own business is National Insurance contributions. Refer to Chapter 15 for details.

Selling up or retiring?

Whether you sell the business, retire, or stop trading for any other reason, you could be faced with revised tax liabilities and possibly capital gains tax. Refer to Chapter 16 for capital gains tax.

Post cessation receipts

If you receive monies after a business has been discontinued and tax assessments have been finalised, you must declare such income under the Income section (Q13) in your tax return. Any 'late' relevant expenditure can be offset against such receipts for tax purposes or as a capital loss, or shown in box 15.8 of your tax return.

Cash basis assessments

It has been past practice for some professions or vocations to prepare their accounts on the basis of their actual cash receipts, effectively ignoring uninvoiced work-in-progress until completion.

This was phased out as from 1999–2000 and any amounts which might otherwise escape taxation will be the subject of a one-off catching-up charge over ten years of assessment.

Personal services provided through intermediaries

The Inland Revenue are seeking to treat workers who provide their services via an intermediary such as a service company, and enter into working arrangements with clients which have the characteristics of employment, as an employee of that client for tax and NIC purposes. This is known as an IR35 situation after the number of the Inland Revenue press release!

The Inland Revenue are concerned at the loss of revenue by virtue of the fact that, for instance, the service company can invoice the client without deducting PAYE or National Insurance contributions and the worker can then take money out of the company in the form of, say, dividends rather than salary, thus avoiding NICs and gaining other tax advantages.

To establish whether you are employed or self-employed for tax purposes will depend on a number of factors, most notably whether an individual invests in his business, risks capital, provides substantial equipment and materials and/or works for a fixed number of hours at another's premises under the direction of a third party – or is free to come and go as they please and, possibly, have a number of clients.

The new rules took effect from 6 April 2000. Each case is judged on its merits and the Inland Revenue will give an opinion if asked. The website at www.inlandrevenue.gov.uk will give you further information.

CHAPTER 15

National Insurance

Unless you can get exemption on the grounds of low earnings, old age or incapacity, everyone has to pay National Insurance contributions. It is compulsory and therefore a further tax on income.

National Insurance contributions

By law, all employers have to deduct a National Insurance contribution (NIC) from an employee's pay over a certain limit and pass it on to the Government, together with a contribution from the employer. National Insurance contributions are levied on your earnings over certain limits and are not allowed as a deduction for tax purposes.

'Earnings' for NIC purposes include pay, bonuses, fees, etc. and any non-business payments made by your employer on your behalf.

There are lower scales of NIC contributions for employees who have contracted out of the State pension scheme and who are members of an approved employer's scheme.

If you have more than one employer or both employment and self-employment income, then at the end of the year you can claim back any National Insurance deductions made in excess of the annual maximum by writing to the NICO Refunds Group.

There are six types of National Insurance contribution:

1. **Class 1:** Earnings-related contributions payable by most employees, including directors. Employers also have to pay a contribution.
2. **Class 1A:** Payable by the employer on most benefits to employees.
3. **Class 1B:** Payable by employers for PAYE settlement agreements.
4. **Class 2:** A flat rate payable by self-employed persons.
5. **Class 3:** If, for some reason, your contribution record under Classes 1 and 2 is inadequate for you to qualify for some NI benefits, you can pay voluntary contributions to make up your record.
6. **Class 4:** Earnings-related contributions payable by self-employed persons and assessed at the same time as income tax. These payments are in addition to Class 2 contributions.

A table giving all the rates for 2003–2004 is reproduced on page 108. Refer to Appendix 2 on page 138 for the 2002–2003 rates.

The Inland Revenue NI contributions office have a helpline for employees on 0191 225 7447; for employers on 08457 143143.

NICs on company benefits

Where taxable benefits are given to employees (see page 52), then any amounts taxable on individuals and shown on their P11D forms are liable to *employer's* Class 1A National Insurance contributions at 12.8 per cent (11.8 per cent for 2002–2003). This additional NIC liability is payable by the employer annually in arrears in July.

The Inland Revenue issue a free guide (CWG5) which shows those benefits that are liable and those that are exempt from this NI charge.

Contracting out

There are lower scales of NIC contributions for employees who have contracted out of the State earnings-related pension scheme (see overleaf) and who are members of an approved employer's scheme.

Individuals may also contract out via an appropriate personal pension scheme and have a proportion of both their employer's and their own National Insurance contributions, referred to as the contracted-out rebate, paid into their own personal pension plan.

Self-employed

All self-employed people are liable to pay flat-rate Class 2 NICs either by a direct payment or direct debit through a bank, etc.

If your earnings from self-employment in 2003–2004 are going to be less than £4,095 (£4,025 in 2002–2003) you should apply at the local tax office to be exempted on the grounds of small earnings.

Inform the tax office if Class 2 contributions are not due for any period (for example, if you are incapacitated). An application for deferral or exemption has to be done annually and *there are strict time limits.*

In addition, you may be liable to pay a Class 4 contribution based on your profits chargeable to tax after deducting any capital allowances.

If, in addition to running your own business, you also have earnings from an employment on which you pay PAYE tax, then you may be liable to pay additional Class 1 National Insurance contributions. However, there is an upper limit on your total liability – ask your tax office for an explanatory booklet or telephone the helpline on 08459 154655.

Statutory sick pay, maternity, paternity and adoption pay

Employers are responsible for paying statutory sick pay (SSP) to their employees for up to 28 weeks of sickness absence.

SSP is taxable as earnings and applies to virtually all employees; there are some exceptions, for example those entitled to the State pension and those on low earnings. The amount you receive depends on your earnings level, and the amount an employer can recover is limited.

From April 2003, statutory maternity pay is payable to an employee for a maximum of 26 weeks. Statutory paternity pay and adoption pay are payable for two weeks at the same rate as SMP. The majority of the payment can be reclaimed from the Government by the employer.

Married women

If you are paying reduced National Insurance rates, it may be beneficial for you to cancel this election if you are on low earnings – that way you will not have to pay National Insurance but could still build up entitlement to benefits.

National Insurance rates and limits for 2003–2004	
Class 1 employed earner **Standard rate** for non-contracted out employees (see note1)	**Employees** 11 per cent on earnings above £89 a week up to and including earnings of £595 a week, then 1 per cent on all earnings above this figure
	Employers 12.8 per cent on earnings above £89 a week
Class 1A On most benefits given to employees	12.8 per cent payable only by employers based on individual's assessable benefit (see page 51)
Class 1B PAYE settlement agreements	12.8 per cent payable by employers
Class 2 Self-employed Small earnings exemption	£2.00 a week £4,095 a year
Class 3 Voluntary contributions rate	£6.95 a week
Class 4 Self-employed	8 per cent between £4,615 and £30,940 and 1 per cent thereafter
Lower limit of profits or gains	£4,615
Upper limit of profits or gains	£30,940

Notes
1. The upper limit for employee's Class 1 and self-employed Class 4 contributions is removed from 6 April 2003 as the additional 1 per cent rate applies to all earnings above the lower earnings or lower profits limit respectively.
2. There are lower percentages for contracted-out employees and reduced rates for certain married women and widows holding a certificate of election (CF383), share fishermen and volunteer development workers.

CHAPTER 16

Capital gains tax

The earlier chapters in this book dealt with tax that may be payable on income (that is, your earnings, pensions, investment income, etc.).

You may also be liable to pay tax on gains from capital (that is, assets and possessions, e.g. land and buildings, shares, antiques, paintings or a business) when such assets change hands.

The taxation of capital gains has always been complicated and, in recent budgets, instead of taking the opportunity to simplify this tax it was made even more complicated by a radical re-organisation.

Therefore, only a concise summary is given here in order to provide background knowledge. If in doubt, seek professional advice.

This chapter deals specifically with disposals by individuals. There are special rules for business assets and interests in trusts, which are outside the scope of this book.

What is a capital gain?

A capital gain is any profit arising when you sell, transfer, give, receive compensation for, or otherwise dispose of any of your assets or possessions. There is no capital gains tax payable on death but instead you may be liable for inheritance tax (see Chapter 17).

Is there such a thing as a capital loss?

Yes; obviously it is the reverse of a capital gain, and any capital losses are deducted from any capital gains that you make in the same year. If your capital losses exceed your capital gains, then you cannot claim tax back, but you can carry forward the losses against future gains.

Can you make capital gains without incurring any tax liability?

Yes. There are some specific assets which are free from this tax:
- Chattels – such as jewellery, pictures and furniture – where the proceeds are £6,000 or less (this limit has remained at this level since 1970!).
- Compensation for damages.
- Decorations for gallantry, unless purchased.
- Foreign currency for personal use.

- Gains up to a certain amount on the sale of your business if you are 50 or over, or retiring earlier due to ill health (but see page 115).
- Gambling, pools and lottery winnings and prizes.
- Gifts of outstanding public interest given to the nation.
- Gifts to charities.
- Government stocks and public corporation stocks.
- A house owned and occupied by you which is your main residence. If part let, see page 116, and for claims for use of your home as your office see page 58.
- Individual savings accounts (ISAs), including the transfer of shares from an employee share scheme.
- Land and buildings given to the National Trust.
- Life policies and deferred annuities (unless sold on by original owner).
- Motor cars (private).
- National Savings Certificates; Premium Bonds.
- Personal equity plan (PEP) investments held for at least a full calendar year, starting 1 January.
- Qualifying corporate bonds.
- Save as You Earn schemes.
- Shares subscribed for under the Business Expansion Scheme (BES) or Enterprise Investment Scheme (EIS).
- Shares subscribed for in approved quoted venture capital trusts
- TESSA accounts.

Annual exemption

You are allowed to make capital gains of £7,900 (£7,700 in 2002–2003) in each year (after deducting all or part of any capital losses) before you are liable to pay capital gains tax. Most trusts are exempt on the first £3,950 (£3,850 in 2002–2003).

In addition, there may also be relief for inflation depending on how long you have held an asset (see overleaf).

How to avoid capital gains tax

The main step to take is to ensure that you are making full use of the 'free of tax' list above. For example, do put some of your savings into ISAs, pension schemes, National Savings, Government stocks, various venture and enterprise schemes.

If you do hold shares and other assets that can be sold, manage them in such a way that you take advantage of the annual exemption amounts.

Married couples each get the annual exemption in their own right, but losses cannot be offset between husband and wife.

Transfers of assets made between married couples are treated as taking place for no capital gain or loss. This does not apply if the parties are separated or divorced. Where an asset has been transferred between married couples, the taper relief (see page 113) on any later sale or transfer will be based on the combined period of ownership.

Remember that your main home is exempt from capital gains tax.

Rates of tax

An individual pays capital gains tax on gains above the annual exemption limit at income tax rates as if the gains were savings added to total income. You may therefore pay capital gains tax at the starting rate (10 per cent), savings rate (20 per cent) or higher rate (40 per cent) depending on your other income, or a combination of the rates may be used if, for example, when added to your other income the gain takes you into the higher-rate band.

Any capital gains incurred by a company are charged to corporation tax, with no annual exemptions, but indexation continues to apply rather than the tapering relief scheme. Trusts have differing rates according to the type of trust and nature of the income.

Can you get relief for inflation?

Yes. In respect of assets held on 5 April 1998 an indexation allowance can be claimed for the period of ownership up to 30 April 1998. Thereafter a tapering relief system will be applied to those assets and to assets purchased after 5 April 1998.

Indexation allowance

The indexation is based on the value at 31 March 1982 or acquisition value if acquired later, so you will need to know the value at 31 March 1982 for assets acquired before then. Refer to your tax office to obtain the percentage by which the retail prices index has increased either from 31 March 1982 or the date you acquired the asset (if later) to April 1998.

Note that indexation can only be offset against any capital gain; it cannot be used to create or increase a capital loss.

Tapering relief

A tapering scale replaced the indexation allowance from 6 April 1998 (see table on page 113). Assets acquired before 17 March 1998 qualified for an addition of one year when applying the taper (except for business assets disposed of on or after 6 April 2000).

The taper is applied to the net gains that are chargeable after the deduction of any current year's losses and losses brought forward from earlier years. The annual exemption amount (see page 110) will then be deducted from the tapered gains.

Purchases and sales within a 30-day period are matched so that no gain or loss will be realised for tax purposes, therefore the practice known as 'bed and breakfasting' has become redundant.

Example of the combination of indexation allowance and tapering relief

A non-business asset cost £10,000 in 1989 and is sold or transferred for £20,000, after deducting allowable selling costs, in March 2003

		£
Disposal proceeds		20,000
Cost	£10,000	
Indexation allowance from 1989 to 1998 based on Inland Revenue index, say	4,000	14,000
Gain before taper relief		6,000
Tapering relief – Five years taper relief 15 per cent		900
Four years plus one extra year as asset was held prior to March 1998		
Percentage of gain chargeable 85 per cent		£5,100

Notes
1. As the asset was held prior to 17 March 1998, one extra year is added to the number of full years the asset was owned. The taper relief available for business assets is greater. If the asset had been held prior to 31 March 1982, the value at that date would have been used as the cost, if it was higher than its original cost.
2. If you elect to rebase the cost of an asset to its 1982 value than *all* chargeable assets have to be valued that way; you cannot be selective.

What is the cost of an asset?

For assets purchased or acquired since 31 March 1982, the initial purchase price (or market value if not purchased), plus expenses incurred before indexation is applied, will be the cost figure for calculating any capital gain or loss.

For assets held before 31 March 1982 you can use *either* their original cost (or market value if not purchased) plus expenses, *or* the value as at 31 March 1982 whichever gives the smaller gain or loss in each case. Alternatively, you can elect to adopt the 31 March value for all of your assets. Such an election, once made and notified to the tax inspector, cannot be changed.

Capital gains tapering relief chart

Gains on business assets

Number of complete years after 5 April 1998 for which asset held	Percentage of gain chargeable	Equivalent tax rates for higher-rate taxpayer
		The figure for sales prior to 6 April 2002 is shown in brackets
0	100 (100)	40 (40)
1	50 (87.5)	20 (35)
2	25 (75)	10 (30)
3	25 (50)	10 (20)
4	25 (25)	10 (10)
5	25 (25)	10 (10)
6	25 (25)	10 (10)
7	25 (25)	10 (10)
8	25 (25)	10 (10)
9	25 (25)	10 (10)
10 or more	25 (25)	10 (10)

Gains on non-business assets

Number of complete years after 5 April 1998 for which asset held	Percentage of gain chargeable	Equivalent tax rates for higher-rate / 20 per cent rate taxpayer*
0	100	40 / 20
1	100	40 / 20
2	100	40 / 20
3	95	38 / 19
4	90	36 / 18
5	85	34 / 17
6	80	32 / 16
7	75	30 / 15
8	70	28 / 14
9	65	26 / 13
10 or more	60	24 / 12

Notes:
*Since 6 April 2000, gains may also be charged at the 10 per cent starting rate, depending on your total income.

How to calculate a capital gain or loss

To calculate any capital gains or losses, you need to prepare a schedule showing a brief description of all the assets you have sold; the date and cost of acquisition; value at 31 March 1982 if held at that date; the date of disposal and disposal proceeds.

The next step is to calculate the 'unindexed gain or loss' but at this stage you must decide the figure of cost you are going to adopt (see above). You can then work out the gain or loss.

If the result is an unindexed loss, this will be the figure you enter in the tax return; if an unindexed gain arises, then refer to the paragraphs on inflation on page 111.

Paying capital gains tax

Capital gains tax is payable, with any balance of income tax due, on the following 31 January each year. If you sell an asset on which you have a capital gain on the 6 April rather than on 5 April you will have an extra year before having to pay the capital gains tax.

Can you defer paying the tax?

There are two ways in which you can defer paying the tax, either by claiming re-investment relief or roll-over relief.

EIS and VCT deferral

Capital gains tax can be deferred by subscribing for new shares through the Enterprise Investment Scheme (EIS) or new shares in approved quoted Venture Capital Trusts (VCT); in such cases the capital gains tax deferral is in addition to the 20 per cent income tax relief.

Roll-over relief

This relief allows you to defer the capital gains tax bill when you sell or dispose of assets in your business, providing you replace them within three years after the sale (or the 12 months prior to the sale). The whole of the sale proceeds must be so re-invested to qualify for this relief.

You can make a claim for roll-over relief within five years from 31 January following the end of the relevant tax year.

What to enter in your 2003 tax return

Remembering that the 2003 tax return will apply to capital gains for the year ending 5 April 2003, if your chargeable gains do not exceed £7,700 *and/or* the total proceeds of sale do not exceed £15,400, there is no need to make any entry at all in this part of your tax return. However, it is wise to keep all your schedules and workings. You may also want to complete the capital gains pages of your tax return to claim a capital loss.

As already mentioned, the capital gains tax legislation is very complicated – only a brief outline has been given here. There are, for example, complex rules for valuing assets held before the introduction of this tax in 1965; there are 'pooling' provisions for identical shares acquired on different dates; there are special rules for business assets.

Inherited assets (chargeable assets acquired)

Contrary to many people's belief *you do not generally* have to pay capital gains tax on receiving cash or assets left to you under a will or settlement. Assets only become liable (subject to the normal exemption rules) when you dispose of them.

Retirement relief

If you are aged 50 or over when you sell or transfer the whole or part of a business (including a partnership) or shares in a family trading company or group of which you were a full-time working director, up to £150,000 of any capital gain may be tax free for disposals after 5 April 2000. In addition, there is a 50 per cent relief on any gains between £150,000 and £600,000 (see table below).

Taper relief		
*Year	*100 per cent relief on gains up to:*	*50 per cent relief on gains between:*
2000–2001	£150,000	£150,001–£600,000
2001–2002	£100,000	£100,001–£400,000
2002–2003	£50,000	£50,001–£200,000

Notes
*During this period taper relief will be available on any gains which remain chargeable after allocation of retirement relief.

Gains on assets you own personally but allow your trading partnership or company to use rent free can also attract the retirement relief provided the sale of the assets is linked to a withdrawal or partial withdrawal from the business activities.

If you have to retire before your 50th birthday due solely to ill health, then you can still qualify for the relief.

In order to take advantage of the full relief, you must have been in business continuously for ten years up to the sale or transfer.

However, an appropriate percentage of the relief is given as long as you have owned the business or shares for at least one year.

Note, however, that this retirement relief is being phased out and replaced by taper relief by reducing the exemption levels.

It will, therefore, be seen that the year ending 5 April 2003 was the last year in which you could dispose of your business and qualify for retirement relief.

For 2003–2004 onwards, the tapering relief table for business assets on page 113 will apply.

Selling your house

Any profit you make on selling the property you own and live in is free from capital gains tax. Where you own two houses at the same time as a result of not being able to sell the first, no capital gains will arise on either house provided you sell the first house within three years. See page 74 for divorced persons.

Many people worry that if they let part of their home, then they will have to pay capital gains tax on part of the profits they make when it is sold. In fact, you can claim letting relief to reduce any capital gains liability.

You need to work out what proportion of the let part of the property bears to the total and apply this to any capital profit. Against that profit you can claim capital gains tax letting of the lower of £40,000 or the apportioned gain before any capital gains tax liability is assessed.

The last three years of ownership of your home always counts as a period of residence, so if you move out and let the property during that time it will not affect your exemption.

CHAPTER 17

Inheritance tax

Most of the chapters in this book have dealt with tax payable on your income. Chapter 16 dealt with tax payable on capital items (capital gains tax) when such assets change hands during your lifetime.

Having paid all such liabilities, you are still not free of the tax inspector, for inheritance tax may have to be considered. Inheritance tax may be payable not only on the value of your estate on death, but also on lifetime gifts.

Most taxes have complex rules and provisions, mainly to avoid fraud, and this tax is certainly no exception. In this book it is only possible to deal broadly with the main provisions and exemptions. You should consult an accountant or solicitor if you need specific planning advice, or you have to deal with someone else's estate.

Inheritance tax payable on death

When you die, the tax inspector regards you as having made a transfer of your estate and it will be valued accordingly.

Certain legacies are allowed as a deduction from the value, however, and this includes:

1. Legacies for the benefit of the nation or for the public benefit, including funds to maintain historic property.
2. Legacies between husband and wife, provided both are domiciled in the UK.
3. Legacies to a charity.
4. Legacies to political parties.
5. Legacies of certain heritage property and woodlands.

In addition, the value of any lifetime gifts which were either chargeable lifetime gifts (see page 119) or gifts that have become chargeable because death has occurred within seven years will be added to the value of your estate on death. (These gifts are *valued at the time they were made* rather than the value at the date of death.)

Inheritance tax payable on lifetime gifts

There are three types of lifetime gift: specifically exempt gifts, gifts that *may* be exempt, and chargeable lifetime gifts.

Specifically exempt gifts

The following are gifts which are exempt:

1. All gifts between a husband and wife, provided both are domiciled in the UK.

2. Gifts up to a total of £3,000 in any one year plus any unused amount of the previous year's exemption. (You can carry over unused relief for a maximum of one year.)

3. In addition to the £3,000 referred to above, individual gifts not exceeding £250 each to different persons in any one tax year are exempt.

4. Additional gifts may be exempt if a person makes them as part of normal expenditure made out of income.

5. Gifts arranged beforehand in consideration of marriage as follows:

Inheritance tax on wedding gifts	
Giver	*Gift limit* £
Bridegroom to bride or vice versa	2,500
Parents of either	5,000
Grandparents or remoter ancestors of either	2,500
Any other person	1,000

6. All gifts to political parties, or UK established charities.

7. Lump sums received from a pension scheme on death or retirement if used to purchase a pension for yourself or dependants.

8. Gifts for the benefit of the nation or public, e.g. universities, the National Trust.

9. Maintenance payments to ex-husbands or wives.

10. Reasonable gifts to support a dependant relative.

11. Gifts for the education and maintenance of your children, if under 18.

Gifts that may be exempt

Gifts to individuals (other than those in the exempt list above), gifts into accumulation and maintenance trusts, and gifts into trust for the disabled are also exempt from inheritance tax *provided they are not made within seven years of death*. These are called potentially exempt transfers.

If inheritance tax is payable due to the death occuring within seven years, there is a tapering relief from the full tax rate.

Chargeable lifetime gifts

Generally speaking, these are all other gifts not covered above (which effectively means transfers to a discretionary trust) and inheritance tax is payable to the tax inspector at the time a gift is made, once the total value of such gifts made within any seven-year period goes above the nil tax band. In these cases, the tax rate payable is one half of the full inheritance tax rate.

The tax is usually paid by the person receiving the gift, although it can be paid by the donor.

Rates of inheritance tax

Inheritance tax rates			
From 6 April 2003		*From 6 April 2002*	
Percentage tax rate	*Chargeable transfer £*	*Percentage tax rate*	*Chargeable transfer £*
Nil	255,000	Nil	250,000
40	Over 255,000	40	Over 250,000

Tapering relief rates					
Years between gift and death:	0–3	3–4	4–5	5–6	6–7
Percentage of full charge at death rates:	100	80	60	40	20

There are special valuation rules and reduced rates of tax for business property and agricultural property, certain gifts to preservation trusts, historic houses and works of art.

Quick succession relief

Broadly, if a second death was within one year of the first death, the second tax bill is reduced by the ratio that the value of the estate on the first death bears to the value at the second death, to which must be added any inheritance tax paid on that first death.

If there was more than one year between the two deaths, the calculation is reduced by 20 per cent for each complete year.

Who pays the inheritance tax?

It is the responsibility of the executors of a will to pay any taxes due before distributing the assets to the beneficiaries, but in respect of gifts made within seven years of death, the executors could ask the person who received the gift to bear any inheritance tax that may apply to it, unless there was a clause in the will specifically authorising the estate to bear all the taxes arising.

If it looks likely that your estate will be liable to inheritance tax, then you should take out term life assurance to cover any likely liability; this should be written in trust so that it is outside the estate on death.

Small businesses

Over the past few years, most budgets have extended reliefs to reduce the impact of inheritance tax on the transfer of interests in small business and agricultural concerns.

In respect of sales or disposals on or after 10 March 1992, inheritance tax was abolished on interests in unincorporated businesses; holdings in unlisted and USM (unlisted security market) companies; owner-occupied farmlands and farm tenancies.

There is a 50 per cent relief for controlling holdings in quoted companies and on certain business assets owned by partnerships and interests in possession.

The rules, regulations and conditions, both as regards the type of business and period of ownership prior to death, are numerous and complex. It is important to consult professional advisers when considering such matters.

Wills

You should always make a will regardless of how much you own. This will prevent your dependants being unduly troubled and will mean that your wishes will be carried out legally and properly. Although there are do-it-yourself will packages available, it does not cost a lot to go through a solicitor, and you will then have expert, experienced advice on which to draw.

If you don't leave a valid will, you will be regarded as having died intestate and your assets will be distributed under strict legal rules, which may not be what you intended.

If you are not sure what to do with your estate, then you can set up a discretionary trust in your will, appoint trustees, and they will have two years in which to give away your assets; you will doubtless have discussed your general intentions with your selected trustees during your lifetime, so that they have a good idea of your wishes.

Many people make reference to specific charities in their will, stating to whom they would like to make legacies. The only problem with this is that if you wish to change the charities you have selected, you have to make a new will.

You can get over this by leaving the legacies to the Charities Aid Foundation, giving them a list of the charities you wish to benefit. You can then change this list at any time, thus saving you the legal costs of changing your will.

If a husband and wife jointly own their home, consider holding the property as tenants in common rather than as joint tenants; that way half can be passed on to the children on the death of one of the parents; with a joint tenancy the surviving parent will take the one half automatically, despite any intention to the contrary that may be stated in the will.

The various law societies have lists of solicitors who specialise in wills and probate. In England and Wales the helpline is 0870 606 6565, in Scotland 0131 226 7411 and in Northern Ireland 028 9023 1614.

Trusts

Putting money into trust can help reduce inheritance tax as it is considered a gift, provided you survive for seven years.

The simplest form is a bare trust but there are also accumulation and maintenance trusts for more comprehensive planning. It is essential to consult an accountant or solicitor as the tax ramifications can be complicated.

CHAPTER 18

Money matters

As well as taking care of your family tax affairs, it is a good idea to know some of the best kinds of financial planning available, not only for the present but also for the future.

If you are married, refer to Chapter 10 to ensure that you have allocated investments between husband and wife to make the best use of the tax system.

Savings and investment opportunities (see also Chapter 13)

Building society deposit or share accounts
These combine safety with easy access and a flexible rate of interest. They are particularly useful if you are saving for eventual house purchase as building societies tend to give preference to existing investors.

Interest is paid after having the tax deducted at the savings rate of 20 per cent. If your total income is unlikely to exceed your personal allowance you can fill in form R85, and once the building society receive this completed form they will pay interest gross.
Note, however, that cash windfalls on a building society takeover/conversion are liable to capital gains tax; a cash windfall on a merger is liable to income tax.

Bank deposit accounts
Banks are now more flexible in the variety of deposit accounts and interest you can have to suit your particular needs. The interest has tax deducted at the savings rate of 20 per cent, but non-taxpayers can receive payments gross by filling in the appropriate form (see Building society accounts above).

Offshore accounts
Many people invest in offshore building society or bank accounts in order to benefit from receiving interest gross and paying tax later. Such cash flow advantage can be lost, however, if you have to make tax payments on account during the year under self assessment. Also, there could be repayment delays and local probate problems in the event of death.

National Savings Bank
Like a building society account, this is an easy method of saving, and money is easily withdrawn. Only the National Savings Bank ordinary interest is partially tax free (see page 11), depending on the total amount in the account. The investment account interest is paid gross but is still taxable.

National Savings Certificates
The fixed rate of interest is tax free and is added annually to your capital at an increasing rate over a period of five years. The certificates can quite easily be withdrawn during the five years but you will lose a part of the total interest. Note also Index Linked National Savings Certificates, the interest on which is based on the increase in the retail prices index, plus 3 per cent per year compound interest guaranteed over five years.

Pensioners Guaranteed Income Bonds
These are detailed on page 93.

National Savings Income and Capital Bonds and Fixed Rate Bonds
These should also be considered (see page 93).

Children's Bonus Bonds
A high-interest savings scheme for children under the age of 16. The Bonds can be purchased at any post office. Interest is added on each anniversary plus a bonus on the fifth anniversary (up to the age of 21). Both interest and bonus are tax free.

Tax-exempt special savings account
Anyone over 18 could open a TESSA account with a bank or building society prior to 5 April 1999, after which no new TESSA accounts could be started. A maximum of £9,000 could be deposited over a five-year period.

The interest was free of tax for the first five years provided that no capital was withdrawn. All tax advantages were lost if there were any capital withdrawals. There was a facility for the interest only to be withdrawn, but in that event an amount equal to the basic-rate tax was deducted.

TESSAs were replaced with a new tax-free individual savings account (ISA) from 6 April 1999 (see overleaf).

TOISA accounts
When your TESSA matures you can transfer the capital into a TESSA-only ISA (TOISA) account within six months of maturity and this will *not* count towards the usual ISA limits (see overleaf) – so you can still use the maximum annual ISA investment of £7,000.

Personal equity plans (PEPs)

Prior to 5 April 1999, if you were 18 or over and resident in the UK you could invest up to a maximum of £6,000 each tax year in a PEP in quoted shares or qualifying unit trusts, corporate bonds, investment trusts, preference and convertible shares. The limits could be exceeded to take up rights issues provided that the shares were purchased before the announcement of the issue.

In addition to the above limits, a person could invest up to £3,000 in a single-company PEP.

The tax benefits of a PEP were that any dividends received and any re-invested interest would be free from tax, and any capital gains would be free of capital gains tax.

All-employee share schemes could also be transferred to a single-company PEP without incurring capital gains tax.

PEPs have now been replaced with a new tax-free individual savings account (ISA) but existing PEPs continue and you can still transfer to another PEP provider, but do check the charges carefully before you transfer.

Individual savings account (ISA)

All income and capital gains arising from these accounts is free of tax and the Government will additionally provide a 10 per cent tax credit each year on dividends from UK equities up to 5 April 2004.

All UK residents can open such accounts regardless of the value of any existing PEPs or TESSAs. Until 5 April 2001 you had to be 18 or over to open an account but 16- and 17-year-olds can now invest in cash ISAs from that date.

The maximum investment each year is set at £7,000 until April 2006. Not more than £3,000 must be in cash (e.g. National Savings, bank deposits) and not more than £1,000 in life insurance. In both instances you can invest up to the annual maximum wholly in stocks and shares. Husbands and wives each have their own limit.

There will be no penalty for withdrawals at any time, except that if you subscribe the maximum amount in a year and then withdraw sums, you will not be allowed to replenish the account until the start of the next tax year.

There are two types of ISA – maxi and mini. Under a maxi ISA, savers can spread their money between cash deposits, shares and insurance in a single plan run by one financial company.

With a mini ISA, savers may use one financial service provider for shares, another for cash and a third for insurance – BUT cannot have a mix of mini and maxi ISAs being started in the same year.

If you want to make the maximum investment in stocks and shares you will need to have a maxi ISA. It's all so complicated!

There have been many cases of investors taking out a maxi and a mini in the same year. In these cases your ISA manager will have to close one of the accounts, returning your investment, and you may have to forfeit any tax advantages. The Inland Revenue have, however, announced an amnesty on invalid ISAs – there is a helpline on 0845 604 1701.

Friendly societies

You can invest up to £270 a year in a tax-exempt savings plan regardless of your age, so this can also apply to children (see page 73).

Unit trusts

These are a way for the small investor to benefit from investing in a wide range of companies. Many trusts nowadays specialise in different areas of investment – some with emphasis on capital growth, or income, or overseas companies, etc. You can purchase units directly from the unit trust company, or through a bank or broker. You pay tax on the income and gains in the normal way. (Many personal equity plans offer unit trust investment.)

Finance houses

These are businesses which generally pay a higher rate of interest than the average market rate. It is important to consult an accountant or solicitor to obtain an opinion as to a particular finance house's financial stability.

Permanent interest-bearing shares (PIBs)

These are building society shares which are listed on the stock exchange and are traded on the stock market. There is a fixed rate of interest. They are not as secure as gilt-edged investments or building society accounts, and they are not as marketable when you wish to sell.

Bonds

The bond market is expanding rapidly with many variations such as investment bonds, guaranteed income bonds, fixed-rate bonds, etc. They are methods of investing lump sums. Watch carefully for hidden charges that could eat into your capital and bear in mind that you could lose if interest rates rise and you are locked into a fixed rate over a number of years. Tax is deducted on payment and cannot be reclaimed by non-taxpayers.

Government stocks

These stocks, known as gilt-edged securities, are quoted on the stock exchange. They can be purchased through a bank or broker or through the Bank of England Registrar (telephone freephone 0800 818 614 for a form).

Since 6 April 1998, new holders of all types of Government stocks have received the interest gross. This is beneficial and will delay the payment of any tax, but don't forget that you may have to pay over this tax after the tax year finishes. (If you want to have tax deducted from your interest you can elect to do so when you buy the shares.) Profits on sale are free from capital gains tax.

Ordinary shares in quoted companies

Buying shares quoted on the stock exchange is a gamble, for the share price of even the most well-known names can fluctuate considerably over a short period. You should obtain professional advice before investing.

Dividends are paid after allowing for a tax credit. This was 20 per cent prior to 5 April 1999, but has been reduced to 10 per cent since that date.

If you are a non-taxpayer you were able to reclaim this tax up to 5 April 1999 but since then it cannot be reclaimed and it may be more beneficial to put savings into investments that pay gross interest without any tax deductions (see page 92).

The amount of dividend received, plus the tax credit, has to be added to your total income in working out your overall tax liability and if this takes you into the higher-rate band, then more tax will be payable. If you are a basic-rate taxpayer, there is no further liability.

Enterprise Investment Scheme (EIS):

Under these schemes, an individual can gain tax relief on investments in unquoted trading companies. The main provisions are as follows:

1. Income tax relief is given at 20 per cent on qualifying investments up to £150,000 in any tax year.
2. Gains on disposal are exempt from capital gains tax.
3. There is income tax or capital gains tax relief for losses on disposal.
4. Eligible shares must be held for at least five years (reduced to three years for shares issued on or after 6 April 2000).
5. Relief on up to one half of the amount an individual invests between 6 April and 5 October in any year can be carried back to the previous tax year, subject to a maximum of £25,000.
6. A chargeable gain can be reinvested in an EIS to obtain a deferral of capital gains tax.

7. For eligible shares issued on or after 6 April 1998, the subscription must be wholly in cash.

The rules and regulations governing these schemes are very complex. Do seek professional advice before investing.

Venture Capital Trusts

These were introduced to encourage individuals to invest indirectly in unquoted trading companies.

The main provisions are:

1. Individuals are exempt from tax on dividends and capital gains tax arising from shares acquired, up to £100,000 a year, in these trusts.

2. Income tax relief of 20 per cent on up to £100,000 in any tax year for subscribing for new shares held for at least five years (reduced to three years for shares issued on or after 6 April 2000).

Small company enterprise centre

The Government has set up the small company enterprise centre to handle enquiries on all the above initiatives including enterprise zone investments and allowances.

Community investment relief

Investments made by individuals and companies on or after 17 April 2002 in a community development finance institution qualify for tax relief of five per cent a year of the investment for a period of five years.

Investing in property

Investing in a second property may provide a safe investment over a longer period, even though any profit you might make on selling would be subject to capital gains tax. For tax relief on interest on borrowing for such a purpose, see page 65 and for the tax treatment of property income see page 60.

Remember that if you are involved in a barn conversion, then you can reclaim the VAT on building materials.

Your house and mortgage

Your family home

The three most common ways of financing house purchase are by a loan from a building society, a local council or through one of the major banks or financial institutions.

However, in order to add a savings element in the general financing package consider a pension mortgage. This is similar to an endowment mortgage, but the advantage is that it is very tax efficient, for although there has been no tax relief on the interest element since

6 April 2000, the payments into the pension plan are fully tax deductible at your top tax rate.

However, everyone will be aware of the effect that the collapse of the stock market has had on the value of insurance policies and pension funds, and you need to be more aware than ever that the value of shares can go down as well as up.

Selling your house

Any profit you make on selling the property you own and live in is free from capital gains tax. See page 116 for the capital gains tax position where there is an overlap between buying and selling, and the situation regarding letting.

Charitable giving

There are many ways of giving to charity tax efficiently. There are payroll giving schemes and Gift Aid schemes and these are all covered in Chapter 8 on page 66.

Pension schemes

In general, contributing to a pension scheme is a good idea because:

1. The tax inspector will pay part towards your pension as the contributions are allowable for tax at your top rate.
2. The pension scheme will provide you with additional income to supplement your State pension when you retire.
3. A tax-free capital sum can be taken any time after retirement.

However, as stated above, there is no guarantee that pension funds will increase in value in the short term – they are essentially a long-term investment.

There are five main ways to contribute to a pension scheme.

An employer's scheme

Either your employer, or both of you, can contribute to an employer's scheme. Any contribution you make will be deducted from your salary before PAYE is calculated, and this is how you will get your tax relief. The maximum total payment for tax relief is 15 per cent of your earnings (including benefits in kind). Remember that the 15 per cent relief includes any contributions you are contractually required to make to your employer's scheme. Many employers offer pension provision via a group personal pension scheme where the maximum contributions will be higher since they are age related (see page 130).

Additional voluntary contributions (AVCs)

These are top-up payments over and above the contribution being paid to your main employer's scheme and are also deducted from your salary before PAYE is calculated. These schemes normally offer good value. You do not have to take the benefit at the same time as your main pension, but at any time from 50 to 75 years of age. AVCs cannot be used for lump-sum payments, only for annuities.

Free-standing additional voluntary contributions (FSAVC)

Instead of topping up extra sums to your employer's scheme, you can pay into a separate scheme and deduct tax at the basic rate before paying the premiums. If you are a higher-rate taxpayer, any additional relief would be claimed on your tax return and is normally reflected by an adjustment to your PAYE code number. Again the 15 per cent overall limit applies. FSAVCs cannot be used for tax-free lump-sum payments on retirement, only for buying an annuity.

Personal pension plans

If you are self-employed, or not a member of an employer's pension scheme, you can get tax relief on the payments made to a personal pension plan. As already mentioned, your employer may be operating a group personal pension scheme instead of an occupational pension scheme for all their employees. In certain circumstances you can have more than one personal pension plan, although these provisions were widened from 6 April 2001. The total maximum available for tax relief as a percentage of earnings (or profits if you are self-employed) is shown on page 130.

Retirement annuities

Personal pension plans taken out before 1 July 1998 are known as retirement annuity contracts and are subject to different rules (see table on page 130).

Stakeholder pensions

To encourage middle to low earners to save for their retirement, the Government conceived these relatively simple and flexible pension schemes, the main provisions being:

- All employers with five or more employees must offer stakeholder pensions if an existing pension scheme does not cover all employees (there are certain limits).
- Even if you are not currently employed, you or indeed anyone else on your behalf, can pay into a stakeholder pension (so you could pay into such a pension on behalf of your wife, husband, partner, children, etc.).

- You can make regular payments, or single contributions, and you can stop and start whenever you like.
- You can transfer between stakeholder pension providers without penalty.
- The maximum gross annual contribution for non-earners is £3,600, but employees and the self-employed can pay more, based on their relevant earnings.
- The fact that you are already a member of another personal pension or retirement annuity contract does not stop you from taking out a stakeholder pension, provided the total contributions are within Inland Revenue limits.
- All payments are made after deducting tax at basic rate; higher-rate relief is available by claiming in your tax return.
- The maximum management charge per year is 1 per cent.
- You can take a lump sum on or after retirement of 25 per cent – the balance in an annuity.

If you are a member of an occupational pension scheme (or are a controlling director) you cannot contribute to a stakeholder pension if you earn over £30,000 a year.

Maximum contribution limits		
Age at beginning of tax year	*Retirement annuity premium percentage of income*	*Personal pension plan percentage of income*
up to 35	17.5	17.5
36 to 45	17.5	20
46 to 50	17.5	25
51 to 55	20	30
56 to 60	22.5	35
61 and over	27.5	40

Notes
1. For plans taken out after 14 March 1989, the maximum net relevant earnings figures on which relief is available are as follows: £95,400 for 2001–2002 and £97,200 for 2002–2003.
2. The figure for 2003–2004 is £99,000.

Claiming tax relief

You obtain tax relief for retirement annuity premiums on policies taken out before 1 July 1988 by claiming on your tax return. For personal pension plans after that date, if you are employed, tax is deducted from the premium at the basic rate – any higher-rate tax relief is claimed on your tax return. Since 6 April 2001 the self-employed also pay their contributions to personal pension plans net of basic-rate tax. See page 95 for details on the purchase of annuities.

Carrying back pension payments

In your tax return, you can request all or part of the amount you pay into a pension scheme to be treated for tax purposes as if it had been paid in the previous year, *provided* that you have not used your maximum amount in that year.

In the case of personal pensions and stakeholder pensions, you have to make this request within ten months of the end of the tax year (i.e. 31 January). The contribution must be paid by 31 January and an election to carry back the pension must be completed at or before the date of payment.

In the case of retirement annuity contracts you have an extra year on top of this in order to make such an election; for example, to carry back an amount to 2001–2002 it must have been actually paid by 5 April 2003 and you have until 31 January 2004 to make the decision whether to carry it back or not. You can only make a carry back claim once the previous year's tax has been paid.

Other pension issues

Bankruptcy and pensions

Since 29 May 2000, anyone filing for bankruptcy has not had to include any personal pension fund in their statement of assets, except where fraud could be established. Legislation already exists to protect money saved in occupational pension schemes from creditors.

Part-timers and pension rights

Following recent legislation, anyone who has been prevented from joining an occupational pension scheme because of their part-time status can have pension rights backdated to 1976. Such employees must, however, still be working for the relevant company or lodge a claim within six months of leaving.

Divorce and pension rights

With effect from December 2000, the law was revised to allow for the allocation of pension funds and rights at the divorce date between husband and wife.

Pension forecast

You can write to the DSS Retirement Pension Forecast Unit at Tyneview Park, Newcastle upon Tyne NE98 1BA to get a forecast of your likely pension and SERPS entitlement.

CHAPTER 19

Calculating your own tax and the *Check Your Tax* calculator

If you want to calculate your tax when you send in your tax return, you need to tick the appropriate 'Yes' box in Q18 on page 7 of your tax return.

You can use the 'simplified' tax calculation guide provided by the tax office with your tax return (telephone 0845 9000 404 if you haven't been sent one and you want a guide).

All the boxes are numbered according to the boxes in the main tax return and any supplementary pages that you need to complete, and although these forms look very complicated it is really a question of transferring all the figures into the correct summary boxes and following the instructions to ensure that you do the additions and subtractions according to the sequence.

To complicate matters, you will need a different set of sheets if you have chargeable gains, have received compensation payments, or AVC refunds, but these are mentioned specifically in the tax notes that come with your tax return.

Because the Inland Revenue have to cover all possible tax situations, their working sheets are very comprehensive and lengthy.

You may find it more convenient to use the *Check Your Tax* calculator on the following pages; even if you don't want to do your own tax you may find the calculator useful to check the statements you get from the tax office.

Check Your Tax calculator

This layout is designed for the year ended 5 April 2003 but you could use it for earlier years provided you alter the tax rates and include those allowances that have since ceased (refer to page 139).

Do not include any income that is tax free (e.g. PEPs, TESSAs, ISAs, the first £70 interest on National Savings ordinary accounts or National Savings Certificate interest).

Check Your Tax calculator	Tax deducted	Gross amount
Your non-savings income		
Salary or wages after deducting any pension scheme contribution, payroll giving	....	....
State pension		....
Other pensions	....	....
Benefits from employer (see form P11D)	....	....
Profits from self-employment (usually the accounts period ending in the 2002–2003 tax year) or freelance earnings, after capital allowances and loss relief		....
Casual earnings, after expenses	....	....
Social security benefits that are taxable		....
Income from land and property, after expenses (exclude tax-free rental under Rent-a-room scheme)	....	....
Total non-savings income	(a) £	(A) £ ....
Less: Allowable expenses		
Personal pension contributions, including retirement annuity contribution for this year (exclude any carry-back to previous year and contributions deducted from salary under PAYE above)	....	....
Charitable covenant or Gift Aid donations	....	....
Interest paid on qualifying loans	....	....
Other expenses allowed for tax	....	....
Total allowable expenses	(b) £	(B) £ ....
Savings income (excluding dividends)		
Interest received	....	....

Dividend income

Dividends received (you should add the tax
  credit to this and then show it separately
  in the tax-deducted column) ....

Total savings and dividend income   (c) £ ....   (C) £ ....

Total income and tax deducted   a–b+c=(d) £ ....   (D) £ ....

$$A-B+C=D$$

Less: Allowances claim

Personal allowance/age allowance
  (but deduct any income limit
  reduction if 65
  – see table on page 139)   ....

Blind person's allowance   ....

Income on which tax is payable

  (D minus total allowances)   (E) £ ....

Tax payable

  (see band limits on page 139 and notes below)

  First £1,920 of income at 10 per cent   ....

  Non-savings income

  £   at 22 per cent   ....

  £   at 40 per cent   ....

  Savings income

  £   at 20 per cent   ....

  £   at 40 per cent   ....

  Dividend income

  £   at 10 per cent   ....

  £ _____ at 32.5 per cent   ....

(E) £................   Total (F) ....

Less: Your claim for personal allowances
that are available at only 10 per cent

Children's tax credit ....

Married couple's allowance ....

Maintenance or alimony
(max £2,110) ....

(G) £ ....@ 10 per cent = (H)£ ....

(F–H=I) £ ....

Less: Enterprise Investment Scheme or
Venture Capital Trust at 20 per cent ....
CIR relief at 5 per cent ....

£ .... = (J) £ ....

Less: Tax already deducted (d) £ ....

Tax due (or refundable if this is a minus figure) I – J – d = K (K) £ ....

Note: You cannot reclaim the 10 per cent
tax credit on dividends.

You will need to add to the tax due, any Class 4 National Insurance liability,
any capital gains tax liability and any underpayment from a previous year.
(Deduct any tax repayment already received (D) or any potential underpayment
already in your tax code for a later year).

Allocation of tax rate bands

The sequence in which you calculate your tax rates is critical to the way the tax
system works – refer to the sequence chart on page 83.

You are taxed at 10 per cent of your first £1,920 of taxable income, whatever its
source.

Then you pay 22 per cent on the next £27,980 of earned or pension income, or
20 per cent of savings income, and 10 per cent on dividend income if you are not
a higher-rate taxpayer.

After that, you pay 40 per cent on everything except dividend income, which is
charged at 32.5 per cent.

Car, fuel and mileage benefits

For current details see Chapter Five.

Company car benefit for 2001–2002

The annual tax benefit for 2001–2002 was calculated as a percentage of the manufacturer's list price when new (less any personal contribution up to £5,000), and included delivery charges, VAT and added accessories over £100, unless they were for disabled persons.

The percentages were based on the list price and your annual business mileage as follows:

- List price × 35 per cent business mileage under 2,500.
- List price × 25 per cent business mileage 2,500 to 17,999.
- List price × 15 per cent business mileage 18,000 and over.

This benefit was reduced by 25 per cent for cars aged four years old or more at the end of the tax year.

In the case of second cars, the tax charge was 35 per cent below 18,000 business miles and 25 per cent for 18,000 miles or over.

There were restrictions for classic cars, as detailed on page 49.

Company car private fuel benefits

Up until 2002–2003 this benefit was based on the c.c. of the vehicle.

Private fuel benefits				
	2001–2002		2002–2003	
	Petrol £	Diesel £	Petrol £	Diesel £
1,400 c.c. or less	1,930	2,460	2,240	2,850
1,401 c.c. to 2,000 c.c.	2,460	2,460	2,850	2,850
Over 2,000 c.c.	3,620	3,620	4,200	4,200

Mileage allowances prior to 6 April 2002

If an employee used their own car for *business* journeys, either the employee could claim the *actual* costs, supported by detailed receipts, or claim a fixed mileage allowance.

In addition, you could claim the business proportion of any loan interest incurred in respect of the purchase of the vehicle.

There was no taxable benefit if the mileage allowance claimed did not exceed the limits laid down by the tax office (see below), whether the amount was reimbursed by the employer or the sum was not reimbursed but claimed as a deduction in the employee's tax return.

The 'tax-free' mileage rates for 2001–2002 are shown below:

Tax-free mileage rates				
Business miles in the tax year	*Up to 1,000 c.c.*	*1,001– 1,500 c.c.*	*1,501– 2,000 c.c.*	*Over 2,000 c.c.*
The first 4,000	40p	40p	45p	63p
Over 4,000	25p	25p	25p	36p

There were mileage allowances for bicycles of 12p a business mile and 24p for motorcycles.

Any payment in excess of these rates was taxable. Many employers declared details of such profits to the tax office under the Fixed Profit Car Scheme, in which case you did not need to record details on your tax return. Alternatively, some employers obtained a dispensation notice to cover mileage payments and, again, those payments did not need to be shown on your return.

Any mileage allowances paid to volunteer drivers in excess of the rates above were taxable as a profit and needed to be declared on the individual's tax return.

APPENDIX 2

Pension credit from October 2003

The new pension credit is made up of two parts: a guaranteed income top-up (GITU), which replaces the minimum income guarantee, and a savings credit. The GITU will top up weekly income to £102.10 for a single pensioner and £155.80 for a couple. The savings credit will be at a rate of 60p for each £1 of extra income from your savings (including SERPS, private pensions and savings) for amounts between the basic state pension (£77.45 for a single person and £123.80 for a couple) and the GITU level; above this the credit is paid at 40p in the £.

The effect of this unnecessarily complex calculation is that no further credit can be claimed once your total weekly income (including the credits) reaches £139 (single person) and £203 (couple). There are different rules for disabled persons.

National Insurance rates and limits prior to 6 April 2003

	2002–2003 (2001–2002 in brackets)
Class 1 employed earner **Standard rate** for non contracted out employees (see note below)	**Employees** 10 per cent on earnings above £89.00 (£87.00) a week up to and including earnings of £585 (£575) a week. **Employers** 11.8 per cent (11.9 per cent) on earnings above £89.00 (£87.00) a week.
Class 1A On most benefits given to employees.	11.8 per cent (11.9 per cent) for employers, based on individual's assessable benefit
Class 1B PAYE settlement agreements	11.8 per cent (11.9 per cent) for employers
Class 2 Self-employed Small earnings exemption	£2.00 (£2.00) a week £4,025 (£3,955) a year
Class 3 Voluntary contributions rate	£6.85 (£6.75) a week
Class 4 Self-employed Lower limit of profits or gains Upper limit of profits or gains Maximum contribution	7.0 per cent (7.0 per cent) £4,615 (£4,535) £30,420 (£29,900) £1,806 (£1,776)

Note
There are lower percentages for contracted-out employees (8.4 per cent) and reduced rates for certain married women (3.85 per cent) and widows holding a certificate of election (CF383), share fishermen and volunteer development workers.

Rates of tax and allowances

	2003–2004	2002-2003	2001–2002
Income tax			
Starting rate at 10 per cent	£1,960	£1,920	£1,880
Basic rate at 22 per cent	£1,961–£30,500	£1,921–£29,900	£1,881–£29,400
Higher rate at 40 per cent	over £30,500	over £29,900	over £29,400

Once the starting rate income band has been used, *savings income* (excluding dividends) is taxed at 20 per cent (not basic rate) if you are a basic-rate taxpayer; once your income takes you into the higher-rate band then savings are taxed at 40 per cent. *Dividend income* is taxed at 10 per cent for basic-rate taxpayers and 32.5 per cent for higher-rate taxpayers.

	2003–2004	2002-2003	2001–2002
Capital gains tax			
Exemption limit	£7,900	£7,700	£7,500
Inheritance tax			
Exemption limit	£255,000	£250,000	£242,000
VAT standard rate	17½ per cent	17½ per cent	17½ per cent
VAT turnover level:			
registration	£56,000	£55,000	£54,000
deregistration	£54,000	£53,000	£52,000
	from 10.4.2003	from 25.4.2002	from 1.4.2001
Corporation tax			
Full rate	30 per cent	30 per cent	30 per cent
Small companies starting rate for profits up to:			
£10,000	Nil	Nil	10 per cent
£50,001–£300,000	19 per cent	19 per cent	20 per cent

There is marginal relief between £10,001 and £50,000 and between £50,001 and £300,000, the fractions being $^{19}/_{400}$ and $^{11}/_{400}$.

	2003–2004	2002-2003	2001–2002
Personal allowance	£4,615	£4,615	£4,535
Children's tax credit†	Replaced by child tax credit	*£5,200	*£5,200
Baby tax credit†	Replaced by child tax credit	*£10,400	Nil
Age allowance			
Aged 65–74 personal	£6,610	£6,100	£5,990
married couple's	*‡£5,565	*‡£5,465	*‡£5,365
Aged 75 personal	£6,720	£6,370	£6,260
and over married couple's	*‡£5,635	*‡£5,535	*‡£5,435
Minimum amount	*£2,150	*£2,100	*£2,070
Income limit	£18,300	£17,900	£17,600
Blind person's allowance	£1,510	£1,480	£1,450

*relief restricted to 10 per cent, †child tax credit applies from 6 April 2003, ‡if born before 6 April 1935.

Index